GOD IN THE COMMONPLACE

God in the Commonplace

a 50 day devotional

Beverly ND Clopton

WordCrafts Press

God in the Commonplace
Copyright © 2025
Beverly ND Clopton

Hardback ISBN: 978-1-962218-87-0
Paperback ISBN: 978-1-962218-88-7

Cover concept and design by Mike Parker

Published by WordCrafts Press
Cody, Wyoming 82414
www.wordcrafts.net

With love and joy, I dedicate this book to
W. Earl Clopton
and
Quentin C. Clopton
(Soulmate and Sonshine)

You're safely home. I'm still on the road.

Contents

Preface 1

Prelude..2

The Water Leak Mystery 3

Do You Drive? 6

Nugget of Gold 9

Divine Negotiator 12

Mix Up 14

Lost in the Mall..16

As Soon as It Cools Off...18

Favor at the Fair 20

Horse Friends 23

Fallow Times 26

Open Your Bible–Treasure Awaits...............................28

"I Still Can't See" 31

You Should Have Gotten an Easy Bake 34

My Conscience Is a Beast..38

Don't Say I'm Not Religious! 41

A Christmas Baby..44

Need Prayer? Let's Pray. 48

Wisdom Road and Grace Lane 51

Hoarding 101 54

Hoarding 102 57

Caller I.D..60

Seeker or Settler?..63

Swap Camera 65

Puff. Puff. Pass. 67

Love is in the Details.. 70

An Interlude 73

Settler or Seeker—Part Two...76

Just Across the Street..79

It's the Little Things 82

"Meet Me at the Bench"...84

Imagine That!..86

Where You're Supposed to Be 88

Bird Battle 90

Connections 93

We Can Do Hard..96

You're On the Clock Tic-Tock...99

Did You Hang Up? Are You Still There? 102

Ride or die...104

Favor. Favor. Favor. 107

The Squirrel 110

Lemons and Life 113

Grace...116

Bucket List 118

Comfort at QT.. 121

Sin: Repent or Manage...124

Cap'n Crunch 127

On the Other Side of the Street.. 130

I Was—She/He Was—We Were...133

Shaken, Not Stirred...135

Time..138

Because Q Lived.. 141

Acknowledgements..144

About the Author 146

The introduction to the fifth book I wrote ended with my declaration that "*I will write until I die*"—which happened to be the name of that book. I completed the manuscript for book six, and as I awaited its release and publication (which can take a while), I struggled to begin writing book seven. I'd begun to think perhaps my bold declaration that I would "*write until I die*" might have been an overstatement. For whatever reason the Holy Spirit Muse and I were out of sync. Eventually, I felt I was being led to explore a format different than the writing I had done to date. Daily, I am awed by the grace God shows me, the favor He bestows, the unexpected joys that dot the landscape of my life, and the continual growth of my faith. Usually, these divine experiences fall within my ordinary comings and goings. They are typically unexpected, inspiring, mundane, sometimes comical, often convicting, and always point to God's sovereignty in some form or fashion. Because a day seldom passes without my awareness of His revealed Presence, I decided to chronicle these incidents or happenings with the intention of showcasing how God is indeed ever present in our lives, from the mundane to the sublime; that it is often in the ordinary rhythms of life that we encounter the gift of extraordinary divinity.

"We can see God in exceptional things, but it requires the culture of spiritual discipline to see God in every detail. Never allow that the haphazard is anything less than God's appointed order and be ready to discover the Devine designs anywhere."

~Oswald Chambers
My Utmost for His Highest

As stated, the ensuing chapters are written in a slightly different format than my usual devotional commentaries. Learning to see and sense God everywhere and all the time requires looking at life in a new way. Each encounter with one another or within the routines of daily living presents us with an opportunity to bask in the presence of the Lord and find reasons to rejoice, to smile, to laugh aloud, to shake our heads in amazement and say, *"Look at God!"* or *"There He goes again, displaying His faithfulness and giving joy!"* Scripture comes to life, and we can proclaim with assurance that we "walk by faith, not by sight." (2 Corinthians 5:7 NIV)

May each chapter open your heart and mind to God's extraordinary presence in the ordinary of your life's journey.

Chapter One

THE WATER LEAK MYSTERY

"Many are the plans in a man's heart, but it is the Lord's purpose that prevails."

~Proverbs 19:21 NIV

To say the $356.21 water bill charge was a shock is an understatement. Expecting something in the usual range of about half that amount, it took a moment to process. The gardener had suggested a while back I might have a leak because of standing water, yet the previous bills were in normal range for summer water usage. But "money talks." And herein begins the mystery. First up was the plumber. After doing whatever it is plumbers do, he announced he didn't see a leak, but obviously I had one. And it was within the yard's irrigation system, so I needed an irrigation company. Within a few days, said irrigation expert arrived and went about his inspection. After an hour or so of doing whatever irrigation experts do, he proclaimed he could not locate the leak and that I needed a leak detection company to identify its location with equipment that only they use. They would place a flag on the leak spot so the irrigation company would know where to dig. (Yes, there is such an entity as a leak detection industry.) Thinking that finally we were on the right track to resolve the issue, I was overjoyed when in just a few more days, the leak detection serviceman arrived right on time for the appointment. After listening to my review of matters to date, he went about his work with me shouting, "I'm leaving you in the Lord's hands to get this done," offered as encouragement. Sadly, his efforts were fruitless. Over an hour later he came back to the door to admit he was stumped. His equipment could not locate a leak, though the standing water was a normal sign there was one. He offered to schedule another appointment and bring a colleague along for a second opinion. I agreed. Interestingly, none of the three service repairmen charged me for their efforts or time, saying they had not made a repair so there was no fee. Divine favor at work, surely.

As I now await next week's second opinion appointment, I'm reminded that situations like this one have the potential to test one's faith. When our carefully crafted plans go awry, frustration can have a field day. Disappointment destroys peace. Pity parties turn to anger. It's vital that when times of stress dot our horizon we soak in the suds of God's words. Jesus tells us in John 16:33 that "*In this world you will have trouble,*" but we are to rejoice anyway because He has overcome the world. As His followers, we refute trouble's efforts to drive us to unwholesome and ungodly responses. We recall that nothing is too hard for God, and that as Philippians 4:13 NIV proclaims, "*We can do all things through Christ who gives us strength.*" That includes waiting on His answers to a water leak mystery.

Now, I'm a big fan of mysteries; trying to figure how the story will end using the clues sprinkled throughout the tale as it unfolds. It's a temptation when I can't wait for the ending to flip to the last chapter and read the ending. But these real-life mysteries we face don't offer that opportunity. We must stay the course of trusting God and waiting on His timing to resolve these conundrums according to His purpose. Doesn't Proverbs 16:9 remind us that though we make our plans, it is God who determines our steps? My understanding of those words has matured since I asked Him to be the "Boss" of me.

I made the second opinion appointment to resolve the leak issue, but the mystery of whether there is one or not, and how to address it remains. The resolution of the situation falls within the scope of issues handled by the Boss. My sense of joy is untarnished. I am at peace.

Postscript: When you're the Boss, you make sure all the bases are covered. During this adventure, God has done just that so far by sending rain three times to keep the lawn green and the flowers from completely fading. Say "Amen" somebody.

Faith Footprint: Have you recently been confronted by an issue that had you scratching your head as you attempted to deal with it? Did your faith manifest itself as you waited?

Chapter Two

Do You Drive?

"They will still bear fruit in old age, they will stay fresh and green, proclaiming, 'The Lord is my Rock, and there is no wickedness in him."

~Psalm 92: 14, 15 NIV

These verses from Psalm 92 are highlighted in my Bible. This passage and others that speak to the latter years of life are uplifting. Caleb at eighty-five was, as he proclaims in Joshua 14:10–12, still strong and vigorous; more than able to continue in the Lord's service. As a fledging octogenarian myself, I am comfortable as a widowed head of household. God has yet to tap me on the shoulder and tell me my work here is done. So you can imagine my surprise when a young sister, a stranger, asked me if I was driving.

I had gone to the nearest Dollar Store wearing my Dollar Store tee whose front reads "No matter how bad things get, I'm always rich at the Dollar Store." In the greeting cards aisle, I cheerfully made my selections to send to family and friends. Just as I finished, two young women, both of whom were half my age at the most, joined me. One of them announced they were there to buy a card for a 75th birthday for a family member.

Without thinking I repeated, "75th birthday."

She looked at me and asked, "you're 75?"

"No, I'm 81," I replied.

The look on both their faces was incredulous. "81!" They echoed one another. They continued with the typical comments I've grown accustomed to hearing when I announce my age.

As I turned to leave, the older of them looked at me and asked, "Do you drive?"

That stopped me. "Of course, I drive," I answered. "How else would I get where I'm going?"

"We took my mom's keys when she was 85," one of them stated.

I thought of a dear friend who at age 95 still drives within her immediate neighborhood. I couldn't stop myself from sharing that with the quip, "When I grow up, I'm going to be like my 95-year-old friend who still drives."

As I left them with looks of amazement still plastered on their faces one said, "We're going to be like you when we grow up!"

That made me chuckle.

The incident was humorous to say the least, but it also prompted me to reflect upon several realities related to age. Throughout the history of our Judeo-Christian faith, age, (declared by my seven-year-old grandson when I was seventy-four to be "nothing but a number") has never precluded God's people from serving Him and carrying out His will.

We are familiar with the stories sprinkled throughout the Bible of God ignoring age to achieve His plans. Years didn't seem to matter when we consider the call of Noah, Abraham and Sarah, Moses, the prophetess Anna, and so many others well beyond their septuagenarian years. I recall fondly the ninety-year-olds, and some nearing the centennial mark who were still vibrant members of my church family. Parking oneself in a rocker on the front porch to wither and watch the word go by when one has reached a certain age is in my opinion akin to telling God, "No thank you. Shower your grace on the young."

What nonsense! In fact, Proverbs 20:29 instructs us that the mark of our aging, our gray hair, is our splendor. What better way to walk in that splendor than imitating, as the Lord allows, the lifestyle of an elder like Ms. Opal Lee of Texas. At 96 years and counting, she uses the gifts and abilities God gives her to actively pursue issues of justice. No watching the world go by for her; she's helping to shape it. Kinda reminds you of those elder biblical ancestors whose grey locks did not deter them.

Faith Footprint: If you've reached the "three score and ten" mark and are still counting, the question is not "why," but rather "what?" *What should I be doing during these senior years to walk in the Lord's purposes for my life? Does my living reflect my faith or am I prone to falter when age-related issues spring up?* What can you do to ensure that the degree of your faith equals or exceeds the length of your years?

Chapter Three

Nugget of Gold

"I cried out to God for help; I cried out to God to hear me."
~Psalm 77:1 NIV

God is *"the Father of compassion and the God of all comfort who comforts us in all of our troubles, so that we can comfort those in any trouble with the comfort we ourselves have received from God."* (2 Corinthians 1:4 NIV)

An anonymous quote I read in a devotional classic hurled me back in time some fifteen years ago. It was a Sunday afternoon. Earl and I had visited a new church for services that morning, and my Sunday short ribs dinner with all the trimmings lay comfortably on our tummies as we simultaneously napped and watched TV in the family room. Life was good. Settled in our dream home close enough to our son and his family so that we could see our grandkids was icing on the retirement cake. We looked forward to the next twenty years or so with serenity and contentment.

Nothing portended that in the twinkle of an eye, and without a word of warning, trouble was about to wreak havoc on our little domestic scene. Few words can describe my fear and desolation as I watched with no ability to turn the tide as my beloved spouse's body was wracked by seizures and convulsions. Between cries to him to "stay with me," and prayers to God to save him, I waited for the EMT to arrive. As the ambulance raced ahead of me to the hospital, I prayed as did the psalmist in the verse quoted above. All to no avail. Grief had crouched in the corner and when I dissolved in tears in the emergency room, it stood and claimed the moment. Little did I know in that instance that even though trouble comes, knowingly or unknowingly, it *"brings a nugget of gold in its hand."* (Anonymous quote, *Streams in the Desert*)

Time and space lost their meaning in the days that followed. Eventually, I recognized that I had ventured into a place folks called Grief City. Talk about the proverbial "babe in the woods." That was me. Officially an orphan, having already lost both sets of parents, death was no stranger; but this was different. Part of me was missing. I'd been chopped in half, and frankly I hadn't been prepared for the emptiness of that nor the "what now" or what I eventually termed the "business of death." I'm not proud to say that Bible study, church services, and prayer team ministry didn't quite hit the spot. Honestly, my greatest solace came from my eldest brother's whisper as we departed the cemetery to "Read the Book of Job one chapter a day for next 40 days," and a 70-day devotional book my daughter-in-law gave me titled *Grieving the Loss of Someone You Love*. I maintained my sanity during that initial sojourn in Grief City by following their advice. Those two disciplines added to my exhortations in prayer for God to help me and to hear me led eventually to being able to find my way through those winding paths of grief. As I emerged from the blanket of numbness that had been my cover, I found my way to the church's grief counseling sessions. There, the leader, and members who had been or were in the various stages of grieving became God's angels to me. Their personal stories and words of encouragement and kindness pointed me to the path leading away from Grief City.

But this was not the only "nugget of gold" inlaid in the trouble known as "grief." No, the real golden nugget came to be the experiences I began to have in the years that followed as friends themselves wandered into Grief City, their spouses summoned home by the Lord. I was able with God's guidance to offer comfort as God had offered it to me. My experiences and how I have come to know joy and peace as the result of the disciplines God offered me fifteen years and counting ago are glimmers of hope and light to many. My personal ministry of listening, praying, and suggesting what worked for me is the stamp of the nugget of gold my husband's death brought. Unseen at the time, but revealed in God's timing, this nugget defies the enemy's power. I can say without hesitation, *"Where, O Death, is your victory? Where, O Death is your sting?"* (1 Corinthians 15:55 NRVS) Truly, life's various trials are not random. Even the most difficult troubles have embedded purpose. Because we live by faith and not by what we perceive with the human eye, we expect at some point that the "nugget of gold" will manifest.

Faith Footprint: Is there a difficulty, niggling issue, or great tragedy now to which you can point and ask God to show you its "nugget of gold?"

Chapter Four

DIVINE NEGOTIATOR

"Some trust in chariots and some in horses, but we trust in the name of the Lord."

~Psalm 20:7 NIV

Since the tragedy of 911, I imagine many of you have evolved as I have into someone more aware of one's surroundings. Add to that awareness the ubiquitous streaming by media of crime, reality, and documentary productions of society's potential dangers and *voila*, your modern-day urban dweller emerges, some locked and loaded and others like me who take a less lethal approach to safety. That's a wordy explanation of why I decided to become the owner of a spray can of mace and a stun gun. Yes, I'm back in Texas, but no, I'm not trying to be Annie Oakley. As a single person living alone, I just decided it made sense to be prepared, should some evil person(s) attempt to cause harm.

I made the announcement of my purchases at a family gathering of some sort, expecting positive commentary, that my actions were wise, a great idea. Instead, the first response was general laughter, and a loudly uttered, "You bought what?" This was followed by "AB (short for Aunt Bev), "Do you even know how to hold a can of mace, let alone point it in the right direction? You'll end up spraying yourself!" Needless to say, the ribbing continued and became yet another future tale of the escapades of their oldest auntie. I got over myself quickly and soon enough joined in the laughter as they conjured scenarios of me bringing down the bad guy with my least lethal weapons.

When the news broke of the war in Israel as the result of Hamas' attack upon the country, I was stunned as I'm sure most were/are. And quirky that I am, I thought of my little arsenal a few days later, shaking my head at how ridiculous they would have been to the people upon whom the violence had been perpetrated; having such devices would not have spared them. Yesterday, the lyrics of a song popular during the Vietnam War began running through my mind. To paraphrase The Temptations, war is good for absolutely nothing.

As we await what this latest "911" type event will portend for the Middle East, for this country, and the world at large, I am drawn as always to God's word. In it He tells us we will never understand His ways nor His thoughts for they are not ours. (Isaiah 55:8 NIV) The words He has spoken—promises that He made and acts upon in His timing—will achieve His purpose and accomplish what He desires. (Isaiah 55:11 NIV) One thing I know with certainty. Man-made weapons of every description are not where we should place our trust, our hope of avoiding evil. Our hope for the resolution of this latest international conflict must be girded by our trust in God. At all levels the people of God are called to the level of trust spoken by our biblical ancestor King Jehoshaphat in 2 Chronicles 20:12; "…*we don't know what to do, but our eyes are on you.*" In this nation, we struggle to know what to do, as we have struggled in the past during times that try our souls. We wonder what good can come from another war. Yet, we are a nation that identifies itself as Christian. The basis of our faith is our trust in God and His Son. The times are evil. The weapons built to deter that evil are themselves deadly. There is only one negotiator who can bring an end to this nightmare. He is Jehovah God. He alone knows the way to peace. May our eyes remain upon Him as He leads us toward it.

Faith Footprint: On this October 11, 2023, our nation once again faces the possibility of engagement in a war far from our shores. Some of our fellow citizens are being held as hostages. What faith principles will you employ in the days to come to demonstrate you still trust in God in such unimaginable times? Is there a way you can make a difference? Will you commit to it?

Chapter Five

Mɪx Up

"There is a time for everything, … a time to weep and a time to laugh."

~Ecclesiastes 3:1, 4 NIV

Those scriptures capture this day for me. Checking my text messages following prayer time, I read that a "sister by another mother" notified us of her brother's death at midnight. She and her last surviving sibling had arrived earlier this week to be with him. It was but a few months ago that another brother had passed, so they were still making their way through Grief City. My heart sank for a moment until I realized the gold nugget within this sorrow was the brief time of suffering and their presence. Still, sadness hovered.

Later in the day, I sat down to make the first of my Care Calls as a member of my church's care ministry. Each month I receive a list of fifteen to twenty members who are marking the one month, three-month, six month or one year's passing of a family member. It is an outreach to offer comfort, prayers or respond to specific requests during a season of grief. Some of the calls go to voicemail, and I leave a message of encouragement. The calls that are answered are the ones that tug at my heart the most, as their lingering pain seeps through their "thank you." I frequently refer them to the devotional book I used many years ago during my personal sojourn in that place. The pall of death casts its shadow, nonetheless.

Putting aside my folder until the next round of calls, I began preparations for my nephew's visit tomorrow to move bookcases. Pulling out photo albums and a couple of very old yearbooks, I came across the 1990 yearbook of the high school where I was an assistant principal. I flipped to the back of the book where the photos of teachers, counselors, and administrators were featured. And there I was next to a colleague, also an assistant principal. The problem was our names were switched. Underneath my photo the name read Rose Rao and underneath hers was Beverly Clopton. I had forgotten the mix up these many years later. I dissolved in laughter of the memory of the consternation of the yearbook teacher and the staff over it. It was too late to amend. For anyone not knowing us, we would be forever thought to be the other. What made it even funnier in those days was Rose was Jewish American and I African American. For some reason, I couldn't stop laughing.

My heaviness of heart disappeared completely, replaced as I sent a pic of the page to family and friends, with the sense that such a mix up will never occur with my Savior. As my shepherd, He knows me by name, or as He says in the Gospel of John, "*I know my sheep and my sheep know m*e." (John 10:14 NIV) Scripture tells us that God knows the stars by name. (Isaiah 40:26 NIV). Distinguishing those who follow Him is surely a piece of cake. No matter the times of sadness that are inevitable in a fallen world, it is a joy to know that the Lord I serve knows me by sight, never confuses me with somebody else, knows the number of hairs on my head (which is getting less an effort I imagine as my hair thins!), and knows what I'm going to say before a word is on my tongue. And most amazingly He knows my heart. I can chuckle at that long ago mix-up even more as it reminds me that I am known by the One who draws the image of what we will look like long before we first draw a breath and will never forget it. That calls for a "Hallelujah."

Faith Footprint: Try reducing the stresses of life each day by finding something to laugh at; something that shifts your focus, even for a little while, from your grief and problems to the joys God offers. Share with a friend.

Chapter Six

LOST IN THE MALL

"For the Son Man came to seek and save what was lost."
                              ~Luke 19:10 NIV

During my yearly summer trip to the Los Angeles area for my "Cali Fix," two sister-friends and I indulge in one of our traditional excursions: the outing to the Fox Hills Mall (The shopping center has a new name now, but for us it will forever be the FH Mall). Granted the mall has declined, with closed anchor stores shutting their doors, replaced by smaller retailers, artisans and shops never heard of back in the day. But still we go. The pull of the place as once a shopping mainstay of the community is hard to shake off, as are the memories of what once was. This year it turned into more a nostalgic wandering in and out of these shops that catered to a new demographic, with only Macy's luring the credit cards from our handbags. We ended the afternoon with a visit to a "pop-up" shop that sold various African American creations by local artists before heading to Panda Express. With their usual indecision about what to order, and subsequently holding up the line, I thought how like little old ladies we were at that moment. I hung back a bit. They've come to know my stock phrase, "You know I don't like old people." And to respond to it with, "says the one who's the oldest of us all." To which I retort, "True, but I don't act old!" The exchange always produces a moment of merriment.

Finally, with orders in hand, we were ready to head out. Lena drove, so we followed her lead back to the car. Up the escalator and out of the exit leading to the parking lot began what would become an increasing wandering into the maze of the three-tiered lot. For the next thirty minutes, if not more, we retraced our steps, in and out the various exits at the different levels. Growing more and more frustrated, I hung back until Donna looked around and said, "She's trying to not be associated with us cause we're acting old!" She was right. I was. How was it possible for three college educated women to be lost in a mall they'd been in and out of for forty-plus years? Ridiculous! We were truly lost!

Thankfully, our guardian angels took mercy on us and on Lena's 100th pressing of the key fob (I made up that number. It seemed like it could have been that many), we saw the lights of her car. We laughed at ourselves on the ride back. How in the world had we managed to get lost?

I thought about that mall experience not so long ago, and how applicable to life in general it is in many ways. As believers we are often like the "three musketeers" above. We know the Lord as our Savior; we seek daily to live the tenets of the faith we profess; we know the what, the where, the how of Christianity, and yet like my sister-friends and I in the maze of the ordinary we lose our way. Challenges of all kinds, our own or those of loved ones, disorient us. The trust we know as foundational to faith fades. Blindly, we grope through the aisles of indecision, wrong choices, our own solutions, never sure if we're in the right place. We circle in and out of the levels of faith pushing our prayer fob in vain. Increasingly sinking into the paralysis that leads to hopelessness, the antithesis of faith, we cry out, "Help me, Lord. I am lost." But soon, like the prodigal son, we come to our senses. We seek the source of our being, our heavenly Father who waits for us to look to Him, to follow Him as He leads us from the darkness of our struggle into the light of His grace; onto the level where He mercifully guides us out.

I hope to never repeat that mall experience, but if somehow, I do find myself in similar straits, not sure which way to go, not sure where the "car" is, my prayer is that I will instantly remember who does; and in that moment seek Him.

Faith Footprint: Describe a time when you lost your way and struggled to get back under the umbrella of God's grace. What helped you get there?

Chapter Seven

As Soon as It Cools Off

"The harvest is past, the summer has ended, and we ae not saved."
~Jeremiah 8:20 NIV

*I*n four more days, the month of October will pass into history for another year, giving a nod to November, the final month of Autumn. The preceding months with their extreme heat and record high breaking temperatures were beyond anything I've known. Yes, I grew up in the state of Texas, but the weather then is not the weather now. The only respite was wherever the AC was—your house, your car, stores, doctor's offices. If an air conditioner was in place and on, you could manage.

I hold a gym membership and had been going regularly to classes designed for those of my generation, older but still active denizens of the community. When we were in the clutches of Winter's grip, I rationalized it would be safer to stay in and wait until Spring came to get back into my gym routines and to my walking in the neighborhood. Spring came, yielded its reign to Summer, and still, I did not don my exercise outfits. My rationale for my continued languishing in slothfulness was the heat. My withdrawal from exercise was absolute. "*It's too hot,*" I'd moan to anyone who asked. But the gym is air conditioned, someone would remind me. My retort: "*Yeah, but I'll faint walking from the car to the inside.*" It was obvious I was in classic procrastination mode, delaying what I knew I should be doing. As soon as the weather cooled off, I would get back out there.

With my head bowed ruefully, I admit that despite the drop in temperatures and the early morning numbers quite in the comfortable range for walking, I continue to sit and watch as several neighbors return to the sidewalks. I have no excuses. This is what I said I was waiting for, but I'm not following through.

What is it with this tendency to put off, to delay what we know we should do. Too often this trait spills into our spiritual lives as well. As people of faith, we have an even greater need to reject it. And yet we struggle to do so. Scripture records as far back as the time of Lot, Abraham's nephew, the danger of hesitation in doing what needs to be done. Understanding that God's wrath was about to destroy the cities of Sodom and Gomorrah, and warned to flee immediately, Lot delayed. Had not God's messengers grasped his hands and forced him to do what he should do his story would have had a different ending. (Genesis 19:12–17 NIV) The writer of Psalm 119:60 (NIV) declares *"I will hasten and not delay to obey your commands."* The God-given and Christ-affirmed commands and teachings stand today. They are foundational to our belief system. Jesus says we are to *"love the Lord your God with all your heart, and with all your soul, and with all your mind"; and "love your neighbor as yourself."* (Mark 12:28–31 NIV) The culture of the times suggests otherwise. Like Lot we hesitate; we delay being the people in the world but not of the world. Our excuses become a bedrock for "isms" that separate, that judge, that turn a blind to the least, the last, the most vulnerable in our midst. We seek vengeance. We elevate incompetence and ignore corruption. Do we know better? Yes. Do we do better? No, not right now. When it cools off, we'll get out there, mix it up and get about obeying God, throwing off the unwanted sin, becoming more fit, looking more like Jesus. Yes, that's what we will do when the challenges of the world cool off.

Faith Footprints: Do you have procrastinator traits? What are you putting off doing right now that you know God wants you to do? Can you make a commitment to doing it? Ask someone to be your accountability coach and track your progress as you grow more into the image of Christ.

Chapter Eight

Favor at the Fair

"I will say of the Lord, 'He is my refuge and my fortress, my God in whom I trust'... Because she loves me, says the Lord, I will rescue her... she will call upon me, and I will answer her."
~Psalm 91:2, 14–15 NIV

According to the International Association of Fairs and Expositions' article "History of Fairs," gatherings in the form of festivals, religious feasts and holy days date back to before the birth of Christ. Both the Old and New Testaments refer to them. Religious activity and commerce merged and beginning in the early Christian era, the church sponsored them on feast days. But as time evolved the "fairs," excepting the church bazaars, became solidly secular. What is thought to be the first modern-day fair was held in Windsor, Nova Scotia in 1765. Today, as noted in the article, 2,000 or more state fairs are held in North America. The State Fair of Texas holds the distinction of being the largest. Yearly, 2.25 million visitors walk the grounds there, taking selfies with Big Tex, the fair's 55-foot-tall statue and icon.

A few weeks ago, two of my sisters and I were among that number. It was my second time going since I relocated here three years ago. We went on a Thursday, the day when admission for 60-plus-year-olds is only $5. Oh, the joy of senior perks! After my many years residing in other states, I, more than them, probably reveled in the sights, sounds and smells, the midway attractions. Candied apples, cotton candy, hot dogs, funnel cake, games manned by vendors shouting for you to try your luck and win a prize, conjure memories that rest dormant until the weather starts to cool and September–October stretch their limbs and say, "it's Fair time." Admittedly, a lot has changed over sixty odd years: demographics are different, more diversity in food offerings, more daring rides, open air concerts that I don't recall being a feature, new exhibit halls, electric vehicles for mobility-challenged individuals.

We sauntered along the midway, having decided to visit first the auto show and African American Museum; then circle back to the food court; catch the band's jam; and cap the day playing games. Little did we know the Lord had a twist to those plans; a test of my profession of faith waiting for me in the least likely place.

There's one thing you need to know about the Texas State Fair. It's huge. The grounds total 12 million square feet, 277 acres with 200 covered in concrete. Directional signage helps but finding your way takes a minute, or two, or three. You get my drift. Stopping to say hello to church members and friends is part of the ambience of fair time; that day was no exception. The auto show was so-so; we discovered the car we most wanted to see stopped participating after the pandemic shut down of 2020. The art museum made up for the disappointment. One of the volunteers happened to be Lillie's church member, and her name was Lena, the name of one of my dear sister-friends. We hit it off! Eventually, we took our leave, famished and ready to enjoy something in the food court. As we found our seats, I reached into my back pocket for my phone. Nothing was there. Neither was it in my purse. It took less than a minute and I remembered. It was on the ledge in the women's restroom where I had placed it when we stopped before departing the museum. Two things happened simultaneously. I lost my appetite for the hamburger and fries I'd just placed on the table and replaced it with a hunger for the substance only the Lord can give. "Stay here," I said, as I turned and began walking. "I left my phone at the museum; I have to get it." I caught just a glimpse of their startled expressions as I hurried away. It was the longest walk I've taken in a long time. I prayed the entire time for the Lord to send a good Samaritan who would find the phone and turn it in. I added that if that wasn't His will, that He would give me the grace to accept the alternative. Over and over, I thanked Him for His mercy and His grace, and for the simple act of being able to recall where the phone had been. Never was there a more welcome sight than the museum doors. Lena was in the place where I'd last seen her, and she looked up with a smile when I approached and asked if anyone had turned in a cell phone. She spoke not a word but pointed to a volunteer at the other table. I turned toward her, and she began unwrapping a phone—my phone. With a smile, she said, "What's it worth to you?" before handing it over.

No, I didn't cry. What I did do on that long walk back to the food court (longer this time because I got turned around and was lost for a while) was utter thanksgiving and praise to God for His mercy, His grace, and His favor. For surely that was what I had experienced. The odds of someone turning in an iPhone rather than keeping it seldom favor the owner of said phone. I remembered Psalm 91, a mainstay of my daily devotional time. The verses quoted above flooded my mind. I do indeed serve a God who is a promise keeper. I recovered my phone only because of His favor. I hope I passed the test.

Faith Footprint: Share a challenging experience during which God's word has proven true for you.

Chapter Nine

Horse Friends

"It is for freedom that Christ has set us free."
~Galatians 5:1) NIV

A well-traveled six lane street divides the section of the city in which I live. On my side a sprawling new community continues under construction, the once rural area of trees and creeks giving way to homes, recreation centers, swimming pools, walking trails and other amenities. The street on which I live is for the moment the last one completed in this section; but earth movers and other construction vehicles behind me are busily laying pipes and streets for future dwellings. I marvel at the serenity of the community, the sense of peacefulness it exudes despite and amidst the activity of the ongoing changes to the landscape. On the opposite side of the six-lane avenue a sprawling horse ranch holds its own. The ranch house and other buildings sit far away from the street. A long running fence stretches the length of the property. Time stands still there. As the hustle and bustle of the urban invades this former area of rural living, a reminder of those times greets me as I wait at the light to emerge onto the street from the subdivision. Five horses often stand munching the grass, slowly moving around the spread of the land. There were eight of them when I first moved here a few years ago, but three disappeared.

Over time, I came to look forward to seeing them, and if they weren't there to stretch and see if perhaps, they were further back on the property. Sometimes I could spy them there or bunched together under some trees off to the side. Often, they stood right upon the fence watching as if waiting for someone to open the gate for them to leave. Quirky that I am I have grown to enjoy these brief moments when they and I are cast together on life's stage; the Old World and the New juxtaposed for a minute or two. To the amusement and head shaking of family, I started calling them "my horse friends," and speaking to them as if they could hear me. I imagined them watching and hoping I was the one who might open the gate to their freedom. "No," I say sometimes as I drive by. "I can't free you. You're not mine." This response to the horses is so unlike me. I don't own a pet and nor do I wish to. You'd never call me an animal lover. They have their place, I'm sure, but it's not with me. I attempted decades ago to be a dog owner, but I failed.

Lately, I've been asking myself, "What is it with these horses? Why am I drawn to them?" All they do is stand around, trapped by forces beyond their control, munching grass and seeking shelter beneath trees or in sheds as the weather so dictates. Surely, the desire to roam as did their ancestors remains buried in their inner being. What prompts this connection between them and me?

Today, the lightbulb came on. My four-legged friends are a visual reminder of the most profound difference between us and them. Though we may find ourselves trapped within fences from which we long to escape, engaged in pursuits not authored by God, we need not wait for our owner or anyone else to open the gate. Christ did that millennia ago on the cross at Calvary. In his moment of glory, He released us from sin and opened the gateway to redemption, to salvation, to freedom. We need not remain huddled, munching on the meager offerings of the secular. The bounty of God's grace speaks through His word. Do you not hear it?

"You my brothers were called to be free. But do not use your free-dom to indulge the sinful nature; rather serve one another in love."
~Galatians 5:13 NIV

"To the Jews who believed in him, Jesus said, 'If you hold to my teaching, you are really my disciples. Then you will know the truth,

and the truth will set you free. …So, if the Son sets you free, you will be free indeed."

~John 8:31–32; 36 NIV

So, go ahead. The gate is unlatched. Walk through it to the places God designed when He allowed your creation in His image. Fenced in places are for horses, not the redeemed of the Lord.

"Many are the plans in a man's heart, but it is the Lord's purpose that prevails."

~Proverbs 19:21 NIV

Faith Footprint: What issues have you feeling fenced in? What are some concrete steps or strategies you can take to break out and live in the freedom God offers?

Chapter Ten

FALLOW TIMES

"Moses went out unto his brethren and looked on their burdens."
~Exodus 2:11 KJV

The dictionary defines the term *fallow* in both its agricultural context and time periods of inactivity. It is within the latter that the story of Moses takes us as he experienced a season of inaction when nothing seemed to happen. After Moses observed his fellow Hebrews being beaten and mistreated, he did what he thought was the godly thing to do to correct an injustice. He killed the Egyptian and buried his body to avoid discovery. Later he intervened when two of his own countrymen conflicted with one another. When Pharoah heard of Moses' crime, he had no pity upon his daughter's adopted son who had grown up within the royal palace. To escape the king's wrath, Moses fled. He spent the next forty years shepherding sheep in a distant land. For this patriarch who would eventually lead God's people out of bondage to the land of the covenant God had made with Abraham, these forty years were indeed a time of fallow. The only action was whatever the sheep provided.

This message that life has its times of fallow resonates with me. I had published my first book, and started the second, buoyed by my relative success of finally becoming an author. About two-thirds of the way I stopped writing. Nothing clicked, and no matter what I did, I could not sync with the writing muse. My well was dry. I noted such in October 2011 in the margins of a devotional book. A time of fallow became my norm, my time in the desert waiting for God to lead me forth. In October 2012, my notation was simple, *"still not writing, just waiting.*" October 2014 arrived, and on the same page of the devotional, I scribbled, "*still not writing??*" How long, I wondered, will I wander in this desert of "no words?" God has sent me here, knowing that I write to His glory to encourage His people. Finally, in October 2015, I penned, "*Hallelujah, I'm writing again.*" My "forty-year" sojourn ended as I realized the message of October 13 written by Oswald Chambers speaks to us today. It's not so much what we decide on our own to do for God, but rather what He divinely leads us to do. He is sovereign in all things. That includes the gifts He gives and those He withholds until we are ready to receive and use them as He so purposes. In my eagerness to write for Him, I forgot that He doesn't need me to do anything for Him; only to obey Him. And as I am more obedient, His plans for me and others proceed as He wills. Moses sought to right the wrongs perpetrated against the Jews. God did not orchestrate his actions. He needed forty years of humility training to become the man who would see God face to face and obey Him. I needed those four years of wordlessness to grow in faith and resilience to fortify my wordcraft so that it achieved God's purposes. And to sustain me in the years to follow that would test me beyond anything I'd yet encountered.

Faith Footprints: Journal a time God sent you into a desert space, a time when you struggled to figure out what His purposes were for you. What did that fallow period teach you about faith?

Chapter Eleven

OPEN YOUR BIBLE-TREASURE AWAITS

"Your word, O Lord, is eternal. It stands firm in the heavens."
~Psalm 119:89 NIV

"Your word is a lamp to my feet and a light for my path."
~Psalm 119:105 NIV

*H*olding second place in my daily morning practices of prayer and dedicated devotional time with the Lord is the reading of the comics section in the newspaper. Since childhood I have enjoyed the humor some of them provide. At this season of life, I find they are often the source of my daily chuckle. Seldom does not at least one of them offer up a reason to laugh and know the lightness of spirit that laughter brings. The writer of Psalms implies that God Himself laughs (Psalms 2:4 NIV); and the writer of Ecclesiastes states "*There is a time for everything… a time to weep and a time to laugh.*" (Ecclesiastes3:1 and 3:4 NIV) Although comic strips in no way equate to prayer and devotional times, I accept them yet as another gift of God's grace.

Recently, one of my favorites, "One Big Happy," really resonated. In it a little elementary age girl approached her mom with a Bible tucked under one arm and some leaves in her other hand. "Look what I found in the Bible," she announced. You can visualize the mother's look of puzzlement as she replied, "Leaves?" "Not just any leaves," responded the little girl. "Adam and Eve's undies." I laughed aloud at that one. And continued to chuckle as I imagined the treasure she thought she'd discovered. The undies of the first man and woman! She obviously knew the story of Adam and Eve and it automatically made the jump to her conclusion that was what she'd found.

We might smile at this example of childhood innocence and naivete, but it reminds me of Jesus' words to the disciples as recorded in Matthew 18:1–4 (NIV):

"At that time the disciples came to Jesus and asked, 'Who is the greatest in the kingdom of heaven?' He called a little child and had him stand among them. And he said, 'I tell you the truth, unless you change and become like little children, you will never enter the kingdom of heaven. Therefore, whoever humbles himself like this child is the greatest in the kingdom of heaven'."

The little girl in the comic strip innocently accepted that the leaves she'd found were the ones with which Adam and Eve covered themselves. She'd opened her Bible and accepted what she found; ancient treasure.

Think for a moment of an adult finding leaves within a Bible. The idea that they were anything other than ordinary leaves placed there by someone for some unfathomable reason would be the reaction. Children more easily suspend the natural and embrace the supernatural; can see beyond the veil so to speak to possibilities adults reject or shun. Children are perceptive; they know the limits of their power; their limitations and helplessness; and learn early on they must trust those who hold that power—the adults in their world. They are humble beings whose greatest desire is to please those on whom they depend for their well-being. In this discourse with the disciples, Jesus speaks to us of what we must embrace if we are to have a place in His kingdom. We need the attributes of children. Within the scriptures God teaches us the ways to honor Him, how to be obedient, what humility looks and acts like. He provides commandments for us to obey and guidelines for our well-being as we travel the road with Him. These treasures await us between the pages of His Holy Bible. He won't make us open it. He created us with free will. So the discovery is ours to unearth.

Today is a perfect day to dust off that Bible you keep on the shelf; to open it and begin to read it with a spirit of humility, suspending your preconceived notions of what it means to truly be a follower of Jesus. Surrender yourself to the leading of the Holy Spirit and seek to look with childlike wonder at the wonders of God's written word, His Google for the faithful, His treasures waiting for discovery.

Faith Footprints: Begin a treasure hunt with the Bible as your source document. Over a period, see how many treasures: new insights, hereto unknown guideposts you can find. Share them with someone.

Chapter Twelve

"I Still Can't See"

"And Elisha prayed, 'O Lord, open his eyes so he may see. Then the Lord opened the servant's eyes...."

~2 Kings 6:18 NIV

A trip to my favorite furniture store topped my To-Do list for the day. I was on the hunt for a new recliner chair to replace two that took up too much space in the living area of the house. Nostalgia dogged me for a while, as this kind of adventure was one Earl and I delighted in back in the day. Soon enough I shook it off, and the thrill of the hunt took over. As I entered the store, a salesman approached immediately. We exchanged greetings, and I told him what I was searching for. I've always had an eye for the perfect piece, so it didn't take long to get the sales transaction underway. Leading me to his terminal to begin the arrangements for payment and delivery, my new "friend" leaned unusually close to the computer screen and began typing. A colleague of his whom I'd noticed hoovering nearby came over and offered to help. He shooed her away and slowly continued. It became obvious that either his computer skills were lacking, or he was having trouble seeing what he was attempting to do. I offered to type in my phone number after his efforts failed, and as I did, the colleague approached again asking if he needed help. He refused again and muttered as she left that she got on his nerves. It was apparent at this point that the issue was not one of his ineptitude, but of his vision. Not wanting to add fuel to the fire, I gently asked if his eyes were bothering him. He replied that he was waiting to have cataract surgery.

"Oh," I responded. "I've had that surgery, and it does make a difference in one's vision."

He answered, "Yeah, I've had them too. But I still can't see!" Taken aback with no quick quip, I remained silent and waited patiently for him to complete the data input. It took a while.

On the way home, I played over the tape of the recliner adventure. As is often the case, I slipped into biblical mode. The salesman's response to a problem that negatively impacted his ability to do his job reminded me of the human condition. The issue wasn't that he didn't know what it took to improve his vision. He'd gone to the doctor and had even completed the recommended treatment—cataract surgery. Yet, as he almost shouted, he still could not see. Is that not a common complaint of we who profess Christ? We've accepted Jesus as Savior, repented of our sins, are saved by His redemptive power, joined a church, worship, read the Bible, pray, serve—and still we cannot see what we thought we would see once we did all that. Our stumbling and flailing continue when life turns sour. We think these attributes of faith aren't working. Can we, like the salesman who awaits another surgery in hopes that this one will cure his ailment, find the answers to our hurt, our pain, our fears? Our sightlessness? Can we stop pecking the wrong keys? The answer is yes, we can.

How?

We make some focused time to sync ourselves with God. We pray and ask for wisdom and guidance. We admit that control of everything belongs to Him. We lay at His altar the baggage we carry that impedes us from seeing and accepting His plans. We merge ours into His. As the pastor said recently, "We leave the details to the Lord." We recall His faithfulness in the past and use that as an anchor for our faith in the present and future. As He has provided, He will continue to provide. We accept that there is no faith without a test; and that it is by virtue of the test that our faith keeps us moving forward.

"Therefore, we do not lose heart. ... For our light and momentary troubles are achieving for us an eternal glory that far outweighs them all. So, we fix our eyes not on what is seen, but what is unseen.

For what is seen is temporary, but what is unseen is eternal."
~2 Corinthians 16–18 NIV

"We live by faith, not by sight."
~2 Corinthians 5:7 NIV

Faith Footprint: Are you still not seeing? Missing sight of the Savior when life throws a curveball that you can't catch? Which of the suggestions above might help you get back in the game with a surety that spills forth and you become one of those whose life is a model of living by faith?

Chapter Thirteen

You Should Have Gotten an Easy Bake

"Do not let this Book of the Law depart from your mouth; meditate on it day and night, so that you may be careful to do everything written in it. Then you will be prosperous and successful."
~Joshua 1:8 NIV

"For everything that was written in the past was written to teach us, so that through endurance and the encouragement of the Scriptures we might have hope."
~Romans 15:4 NIV

Without warning a year or so ago my youngest sister's oven died; gave up the ghost as they say, and refused to do the things ovens are created to do. At first it wasn't that big of a deal. She'd reached a season in which it wasn't used all that much anyway. Like most of us, she had countertop appliances which were easy substitutes. But after last year's adventure of having to bake her famous sweet potato pies up the street and around the corner in my oven, she declared, "I want a new oven."

The months flew by and as the leaves changed hues and the temps dropped, she became even more adamant. Another Thanksgiving was not that far away. The search for the new oven took priority. Last weekend, my brother-in-law spent most of the day installing it. That evening, I called to see how the installation had gone.

"It's in," she said, "and I baked some biscuits." Then she added, "You know it's one these smart ovens. There are so many different things to figure out. I told Dwayne I should have gotten a regular old oven. He told me I should have just gotten an Easy Bake!"

At this point, my BIL as I call him, piped in, "She doesn't want to read the manual and figure out how it works. So, yeah, I told her all she needed was an Easy Bake oven."

I burst into laughter at the thought. An Easy Bake, the little girl's first oven that has a light bulb and an On and Off button. Here she was with the latest in oven technology at her fingertips, but it would not help her be the baker or roaster she was accustomed to being if she was unwilling or hesitant to read the owner's manual to activate her abilities and fulfill the purposes for which the oven was designed.

The Holy Spirit Muse lost no time. "That's another chapter for the book," she whispered. *Yes, indeed* I thought; and here we are.

In the mundane purchase of an oven, God speaks. Consider the possibilities the oven portends for my sister's baking reputation if she will but take the time to read and ponder the instructional guide. How akin to a believer's journey. We've taken the first steps on the road to glory. We've repented of our sins, accepted Jesus Christ as our Savior sent from God to redeem us to Himself. We've been baptized and typically have a church in which we worship. To juxtapose the oven scenario, we've bought and installed the oven and wait to bring its purposes to life. But too many of us are stuck for the moment in the quagmire that envelops my sister. We don't want to read our manual—the Bible—with any regularity, other than on Sunday morning when the pastor asks us to open it and follow along as he reads the sermonic scripture. As it is with baby sister and the instructional guide that came with her oven, so is it with our profession of faith and the Bible which comes with it. This holy manual gives guidance in how to live faithfully. But unless we are intentional in following the directions, we will fail to activate its purposes.

From God's instructions on the tablets that Moses brought down from his mountaintop tutorial session with the Lord and continuing throughout both the Old and New Testament writings, the Bible offers us invaluable insight into how to live as people who are in the world, yet not of the world; people who are doers of His word.

To name but a very few:

"Fix these words of mine in your hearts and minds… teach them to your children… observe all these commands…."
~Deuteronomy 11:18—22 NIV

"Do not let this Book of the Law depart from your mouth, meditate on it day and night, so that you may be careful to obey everything written in it. Then you will prosper and be successful."
~Joshua 1:8 NIV

"Your word is a lamp unto my feet and a light unto my path. I have taken an oath and confirmed it, that I will follow your righteous laws."
~Psalm 119:105 NIV

"… do not forget my teaching but keep my commands in your heart … write them on the tablet of your heart."
~Proverbs 1–3 NIV

"Trust in the Lord with all your heart and lean not on your own understanding; in all your ways acknowledge him, and he will make your paths straight."
~Proverbs 3:5–6 NIV

"Be still before the Lord and wait patiently for him; do not fret when men succeed in their evil ways, when they carry out their wicked schemes."
~Psalms 37:7 NIV

"Ask and it will be given to you; seek and you will find."
~Matthew 7:7 NIV

"Submit yourselves then to God. Resist the devil and he will flee from you."
~James 4:7 NIV

"The Lord, the Lord is my strength and my song; he has become my salvation."

~Isaiah 12:2 NIV

"I tell you, love your enemies and pray for those who persecute you that you may be sons of your Father in heaven."

~Matthew 5:44–45 NIV

"So, in everything, do to others what you would have them do to you, for this sums up the Law and the Prophets."

~Matthew 7:12 NIV

"Do not be anxious about anything, but in everything by prayer and petition with thanksgiving, present your requests to God. And the peace of God, which transcends all understanding, will guard your hearts and your minds in Christ Jesus."

~Philippians 4:6—7 NIV

I'll stop here in the hope that you get the point. Our biblical manual, the Bible, overflows with guidance and directions on how to live the faith we profess. Don't let it lay there unread and miss the thrill of successful living experiences; just as my sister will with her oven when she finally reads the manual.

Faith Footprint: Do you practice the spiritual discipline of reading the Bible daily as a guide or reminder to excel in the exercise of your faith? Or is your interaction with it cursory? Will you commit to a more focused utilization of God's word to enhance the joy available to the those who do? Ask a friend to be your accountability partner as you mature in faith via following His directions.

Chapter Fourteen

My Conscience Is a Beast

"My guilt has overwhelmed me like a burden too heavy to bear."
~Psalm 38:4 NIV

The Oxford Language Dictionary defines the term conscience as "an inner feeling or voice viewed as acting as a guide to the rightness or wrongness of one's behavior. i.e. he had a guilty conscience about his desires." In simple terms, conscience is an innate sense that produces a sense of guilt whenever we act against it.

Not long ago, I chuckled for a week as the creator of the comic strip *Zits* followed the struggle of the teenage main character and his conscience (portrayed in comic strip fashion as a puffy white Michelin Tire character complete with wings suggesting he was an angel) over whether to tell his parents about a party he planned to attend without their permission. For five days the two of them wrestled physically over the dilemma. On some days, the teenager had the upper hand and on others, the puffy character with wings carried the day. Arguments on both sides of the decision held sway until the final two frames in which the conflicted teen stood with bowed head before his mom to confess the lie, he'd so wanted to tell, but his conscience did not allow him to. Pleased with his honesty, she asked what made him decide to tell her. Walking away, he answered, "*My conscience is a beast!*

As the psalmist wrote in the verse above, guilt overwhelms. Our conscience is the inner guide God provides to help us make moral choices to avoid that guilt. A Google dive revealed the Greek word translated "conscience" can be found about thirty times in the New

Testament, with no synonym in the Old. The typical confessor of the Christian faith will acknowledge that conscience is what God gives humans so that they can critique their thoughts and actions. Christians are especially called to be led by this ethereal yet powerful sense.

As our teenage protagonist in the comic strip, we too face situations where we have to choose right over wrong; decide between the quick and easy or long term fix; give up a want in favor of a need; step out of or remain in our comfort zones to help someone; speak out or remain silent as evil holds sway and truth needs to be spoken; downsize the secular and elevate the sacred. This battle with our conscience won't be on display for the world to witness (though perhaps if it were, we might be the better for it). In the recesses of our hearts and the activity of our minds, the conflict rages.

"I will maintain my righteousness and never let go of it; my conscience will not reproach me as long as I live."

~Job 27:6 NIV

"Paul looked straight at the Sanhedrin and said, "My brothers, I have fulfilled my duty to God in all good conscience to this day."

~Acts 23:1 NIV

"They must keep hold of the deep truths of the faith with a clear conscience."

~1 Timothy 3:9 NIV

"Let us draw near to God with a sincere heart with full assurance of faith, having our hearts sprinkled to cleanse us from a guilty conscience..."

~Hebrews 10:22 NIV

"I speak the truth in Christ—I am not lying, my conscious confirms it in the Holy Spirit."

~Romans 9:1 NIV

"Anyone, then, who knows the good he ought to do and doesn't do it, sins."

~James 417 NIV

Our comic strip friend knew the good he ought to do; yet he struggled for a week with his conscience to find a way in which he might do otherwise. Whether in public or private, we do the same. The question is always, "What will prevail?" May an imaginary adolescent point us toward the path we ought to choose as disciples of Jesus Christ.

Faith Footprint: Irrespective of your age, can you still identify with our young comic strip friend who battled with his conscience and eventually yielded? How so?

Chapter Fifteen

DON'T SAY I'M NOT RELIGIOUS!

"The Lord says: 'These people come near to me with their mouth and honor me with their lips, but their hearts are far from me. Their worship of me is made up only of rules taught by men.'"
~Isaiah 29:13 NIV

I decided to continue with comic strip inspiration since presently we're in the season of all things Christmas, and a recent *Peanuts* strip resonates. Charlie Brown's little sister Sally is busily address-ing her Christmas cards when big brother peers over her shoulder. She proudly states, *"Aren't they cute? Each one has a little bunny on it dressed up like a shepherd."* In silence, Charlie Brown turns away and Sally yells at him, "Don't Say I'm Not Religious!"

Of course, this one-sided interaction provided me with my chuckle for the day. In one grand design, little Sally in her mind anyway, summed up what it means to be religious. Christmas and Easter por-trayed by a bunny attired in shepherds' clothing. Perhaps we can give her credit for grasping the rudimentary elements of the Christian faith. Christ was born at Christmas in a manger where shepherds came to see Him, and He died at Easter on a cross; though to be fully transparent, I struggle still with the bunnies and Calvary. Was there a family of them nearby, silently observing the scene? At any rate, the dualism of her drawing speaks to the continuing challenge of believers to live what they profess.

Matthew records Jesus' teaching regarding what it means to be religious in that familiar discourse we term The Sermon on the

Mount when He says:

> *"Not everyone who says to me, 'Lord, Lord' will enter the kingdom of heaven, but only he does the will of my Father who is in heaven."*
> ~Matthew 7:21–23 NIV

For everyone who has accepted Jesus as the Son of God, repented, been baptized, and surrendered to His authority understands His will to be what we read in His word. We know that after we read it, we are called to do it. Ours is a faith that requires action to actualize what we say we believe.

In Mark's Gospel, Jesus confronts Pharisees with this retort to their criticism.

> *"Isaiah was right when he prophesied about you hypocrites; as it is written: 'These people honor me with their lips, but their hearts are far from me. They worship me in vain; their teachings are but rules taught by men.'"*
> ~Mark 7:6–7 NIV

Maybe the apostle James makes the most powerful points regarding what it means to be truly religious, to leave behind the simple imagery of shepherds and bunnies. He teaches:

> *"Do not merely listen to the word, and so deceive yourselves. Do what it says."*
> ~James 1:22 NIV

> *"If anyone considers himself (or herself—my insertion) religious and yet does not keep a tight rein on his tongue, deceives himself and his religious is worthless. Religion that God our Father accepts as pure and faultless is this: to look after orphans and widows in their distress and to keep oneself from being polluted by the world."*
> ~James 1:26–27 NIV

Sorry, little Sally, to burst your bubble. To be religious is to be much more than knowing the story of the Christian faith; of even believing the story of the Christian faith. Being religious means bearing the image of Christ and choosing what Christ would choose should He Himself walk still among us. He doesn't, but God gave us the Holy Spirit to continue what He began; to be our guide as we seek daily to bear the image of what religion looks like in our time, in our age.

Faith Footprint: Reflect seriously on the state of your "religion." When you stand before the Master on that great day of reckoning, will He applaud the way you ran the race He set before you, and say, "Well done?" Or are there adjustments you need to make now to ensure that He does?

Chapter Sixteen

A CHRISTMAS BABY
Cart Before the Horse?

"… God sent the angel Gabriel to Nazareth, a town in Galilee, to a virgin pledged to be married to a man named Joseph, a descendant of David. The virgin's name was Mary. … thee angel said to her, 'Do not be afraid, Mary, you have found favor with God. You will be with child and give birth to a son, and you will give him the name Jesus. … "How will this be,' Mary asked the angel, 'since I am a virgin?' The angel answered, 'The Holy Spirit will come upon you, and the power of the Most High will overshadow you. So, the holy one to be born will be called the Son of God.'"

~Luke 1:26–35 NIV

I think it's safe to say the story of the announcement of the impending birth of Jesus two thousand plus years ago is known to both Christians and non-Christians. The apostle Luke writes in a manner that even the common man or woman, without any formal schooling, gets the gist of this event destined to change the world forever. A young virgin girl, a man to whom she is betrothed but not married, and an infant born out of wedlock star in this divine production directed by the Creator himself.

Roughly 400 years elapsed between the Old and New Testaments. During that time childbirth seems to have been conventional; children born to parents joined in what we term "marriage." With the caveat of a man having more than one wife being permissible and resulting in the births of additional children who were not considered "born out of wedlock." By the era of Mary and Joseph, social mores had obviously changed, with the concept of pregnancy before marriage being a definite no-no, though today no one blinks an eye when a bulging bellied bride-to-be waddles down the aisle, hoping the ceremony ends before the delivery begins. The reactions of Mary and Joseph when confronted with the announcement of the first Christmas Baby coming forth from her, a virgin, suggest that our modern-day event would not have been viewed through the same lens. Immediately, Mary got to the point after the angel announced her conception of a child. "*How can this be?*" she said. "*I am a virgin.*" Modern day speak for "*Hold on. No way can I be pregnant. I haven't slept with Joseph. That's not allowed. We're not married yet. Can you imagine what my parents, his parents, our friends, and the priest will say?*" She knew the social dynamics of the time. She would be ostracized, whispered unkindly about, forever marked. Even the poor groom-to-be had his doubts, and as scripture reads, had decided to break the marriage contract. Divine intervention had to convince him otherwise. These biblical ancestors had not heard the phrase, "putting the cart before the horse," but it was an apt description for what they faced.

In conversation not so long ago with family members, talk turned to the plight of a nephew whose girlfriend is pregnant. The prospect of an impending marriage seemed dim, as this would be their third child. Opinions regarding the situation flew back and forth, often in consternation and a sense of helplessness. Afterwards, I mused about the plight of unmarried mothers, the children they give birth to, and the stigma attached to the circumstances of those pregnancies. I found no reference in the Bible of the term "unwed mother." The first reference to childbirth itself occurs in Genesis 3:16 when God tells Eve that He "*will greatly increase your pains in childbearing; with pain you will give birth to children.*" That Eve was Adam's wife at that time is confirmed in that same chapter, but there appears to be no further distinctions applied to the marital state of childbearing women. With that acknowledgment we can address the question whether distinctions are applicable to the status of "unwed mothers" and the children they bear. Have they as often characterized "putting the cart before the horse?" Are we as Christians called to dig deeper and view them in the light of our Savior's birth. After all, He is the first Christmas baby. His unconventional birth, by man's standards anyway, demonstrated God's sovereignty over everything, including the marital status of His mother. I have come to think that Jesus' birth absent the marriage of his mother sends a powerful message. Yes, without doubt His birth is divinely authored, not of man's desire. Yet, it still is akin to the births of so many whose parents are unmarried when they greet the world outside their mother's womb.

I choose to call them "Christmas Babies." They join Jesus, the reason for the season, as gifts from God for the world. We should reject the identifiers such as unplanned, unwanted, illegitimate because they were born to mothers outside a traditional marriage. God's purposes for humanity are often "outside the box." Ultimately, these "Christmas" babies are born within the will of God as are all who draw breath.

What then shall we proclaim about these uniquely created children? Other than not having parents who were married when they arrive, does anything mark them as less than? The unequivocal answer is, No. They have the same potential to bear the stamp of the Creator. The realization of who such children are and can be must shift the focus from condemnation of such pregnancies and the family dynamics that produce them. The cry of a "Christmas" baby at birth is a cry that announces, "*I am here by God's grace and design. Help me soar into the purposes He has for me.*"

The next time you're tempted into debate or negative opinion-giving regarding mothers and fathers who for whatever reasons give birth to children outside the bond of matrimony, stop and think. You're talking about a baby born as was the Savior of the world. Born before marriage, rejected, despised, yet within God's divine plans becoming the greatest gift ever given. Save your commentary. There is only one Creator of life and the way it comes to be. And it's not you.

Faith Footprint: Reflect upon the idea that children labeled illegitimate because of the circumstances of their birth might well be more like Jesus than those born in the traditional combine of marriage. Is it difficult for you to do that? Is there an argument for my contention that babies worn out of wedlock are "Christmas" babies? Are they "putting the cart before the horse?"

Chapter Seventeen

NEED PRAYER? LET'S PRAY.

"O Lord, the God who saves me, day and night I cry out before you. May my prayer come before you; turn your ear to my cry."
~Psalm 88:1–2 NIV

There is little doubt that prayer or praying is foundational to the Christian faith. The website Tithe.ly reports there are over 650 prayers in the Bible with twenty-five prayers attributed to Jesus. The number of times the words "prayer" or "pray" is used depends upon the version of the Bible one selects for reference. Some might say a person who professes Christianity but who doesn't pray might need a major do-over.

As someone who will call on the Lord at the drop of a hat or at any given moment, I was instantly drawn as I drove down the street to two signs held aloft by a man and woman standing some six or so feet apart on a lawn abutting the sidewalk. In huge letters, one sign read, "Let's Pray." The other asked, "Need Prayer?" With no break in the traffic flow, I had time only to see that these two people were somehow, or another, connected to a faith tradition that advocates prayer. As I continued my way, I wondered if they represented a particular denomination or if they were self-proclaimers; and if the latter to whom were they praying and with what authority? Or were their signs simple reminders of the significance of praying?

Sometime later, my thoughts returned to these two street-side "prayer warriors." They were ordinary in appearance, sans any identifying church affiliation. Belatedly, I wished I'd circled the block and returned to find out more about them and the purposes for their sidewalk prayer ministry. My curiosity had to be settled within my own understanding of our faith about prayer and what our Bible teaches, at least the versions that are my mainstays: NIV, New Oxford Revised Standard, and the New King James.

There's a gospel song that indicates that drawing close to God is often the result of praising Him. I can say without reservation that prayer is what I do when I want or need to get close to Him. Scripture confirms I am not alone in this regard.

> *He alone is my rock and my salvation; he is my fortress; I will never be shaken.*
> ~Psalm 62:2

> *Truly my soul finds rest in God; my salvation comes from him.*
> ~Psalm 62:1

> *Jesus turned and saw her. "Take heart, daughter," he said, "your faith has healed you." And the woman was healed at that moment.*
> ~Matthew 9:22)

Prayer lines and prayer ministries of all kinds proliferate the world of the faithful. I know that prayer is a direct pipeline to the Savior. Whether I'm lifting prayers of intercession, faith, agreement, petition, thanksgiving, worship, or for the help of the Holy Spirit, I know I am under the authority of Christ as I pray in His name as scripture so tells us to.

I don't judge the intentions of the sidewalk prayer warriors, but my hope and my prayer is that what they do they do in the name of the Savior; and that others who may stop for prayer with them are of like mind. For scripture is also clear that not everyone who proclaims Christ really knows Him:

> *"Not everyone who says to me, 'Lord, Lord' will enter the kingdom of heaven, but only he who does the will of my Father who is in heaven."*
> ~Matthew 7:21 NIV

Faith Footprint: Maybe you've had a similar experience to mine. What was your reaction? Reflect upon the chapter and its application in our world today.

Chapter Eighteen

Wisdom Road and Grace Lane

"The fear of the Lord is the beginning of wisdom, and knowledge of the Holy One is understanding.

~Proverbs 9:10) NIV

"Wisdom reposes in the heart of the discerning and even among fools she lets herself be known."

~Proverbs 14:33 NIV

"In him we have redemption through his blood, the forgiveness of sins, in accordance with the richness of God's grace that he lavished on us with all wisdom and understanding."

~Ephesians 1:7–8 NIV

"For it is by grace you have been saved, through faith – and this not from yourselves, it is the gift of God."

~Ephesians 2:8 NIV

As you might have surmised, my imagination is often triggered into overdrive by things others take for granted. Such is the case of my reaction to the street signs that give title to this piece. It was some years ago when I resided in the state of Georgia that I passed Wisdom Road, in Peachtree City, the town that abutted the one in which I lived. I recall smiling to myself and thinking, "Wisdom Road. Who and why would you give a street that name? Is it named after someone? Does it have significance attached to it which gives it special significance?" In my mind those were reasonable questions.

Because I passed the street so often, the why of it morphed into rambling ideas: Were there special requirements residents had to present to move into a house on Wisdom? Were you evicted from the street if you began to demonstrate wisdom's opposite—foolishness? Were their street monitors who made sure all who resided there were indeed wise? Or was it perhaps that buyers selected that street specifically because of their desire to acquire wisdom by simply living on a street so named? At one point I turned into the street just to see if there was anything that set it apart from others in the subdivision. To my eyes, nothing did. Eventually, I made a mental note to consider the street name as fodder for a future writing.

Fast forward to 2024. I'm a settled resident in a Dallas suburb named Mesquite. It's one of those places in which the developers are building new subdivisions as fast as the supply chain can get the materials to the sites. In just three years what was once a 1400-acre family working farm has become the site of a planned community to be comprised of residential and commercial properties, man-made lakes, nature trails, and a host of other amenities to tempt potential buyers. Recently, as I drove down one of the perimeter roads, I saw a sign for a street named Grace Lane. It's Georgia sister, Wisdom Road, popped into mind. Another street bearing the name of an attribute of our faith. Was it a tribute to someone named Grace? Does something divine await the future residents of a street so named? Will they have to complete a "Grace Identifier" form to proceed with the sale? The quirkiness spiraled out of control until I thought, "Stop it, Beverly!"

Settled now, I reflect upon these secular street names we so easily associate with our faith. Perhaps it's just coincidence that I happened upon them. But because I try to be alert to God's presence in everything, I can't help wondering if it is more than that. In the fifteen years that I lived in the Atlanta area, I think in hindsight that Wisdom Road was positioned where I would see it regularly as I drove to and from my destinations. As Proverbs 8: reads, "Does not wisdom call out… on the heights along the way, where the paths meet, she takes her stand…" That is why I believe the Wisdom Road sign was so placed; to serve as a frequent reminder to me that God's wisdom was an attribute I needed more of each day. I believe God hoped if I saw the word often enough, I would grow in the acquisition of it. I would mature into one who listens more and more to His instructions and be wise because of so doing. I would be blessed, find life, and receive favor from Him (Proverbs 8:34—35 NIV)

Having come to such a conclusion regarding the Wisdom Road sign, I think the Grace Lane sign also has a message. Now, I've only seen it once. But unlike Wisdom Road, once is enough. I understand that God's grace is not something I aspire to obtain. I have it already. From the moment Jesus willingly went to the cross and sacrificed His life for humanity, His grace has flown to all who believe in and strive to obey Him as the expression of that belief. The street sign Grace Lane simply reconfirms what I know. God's grace was, is, and will be for me more than sufficient for whatever He allows me to face.

Who would think an ordinary street sign could herald a divine message? I wager not your average Joe or Josephine. Learning to sense God's presence in the ordinary things of life, the secular stuff that may seem to have no connection to the divine is a spiritual discipline worthy of pursuit. Want to marvel at the miracles He authors daily? Take the time to search for His majesty. He's everywhere all the time.

Faith Footprint: Look for the divine wonders God places in your secular environment. Be deliberate at seeing His hand in situations or experiences that on the surface seem unrelated to the secular. Share them.

Chapter Nineteen

HOARDING 101

"I have seen a grievous evil under the sun: wealth hoarded to the harm of its owner..."
~Ecclesiastes 5:13 NIV

"Do not store up treasures on earth, where moth and rust destroy. ... For where your treasure is, there your heart will be also."
~Matthew 6: 19, 21 NIV

*O*nce again, my daily dose of comic strip humor prompts a reflection that fuels my contention that our Lord operates in every area of our lives and that His word has something to offer in any situation. The parents in a comic strip were busily cleaning out the garage when the wife commented that the shelves were especially messy. The husband asks where all the stuff came from, and she answers, *"The pandemic. Remember."* In the concluding panel, the two of them stare at the countless rolls of toilet paper that were the cause of the messy shelves. The wife commented she had not had to buy tissue since 2020, and he responded, *"Maybe we over-prepared."*

This is that "duh" moment when someone says. *"You think,"* in that tone often intended to convey sarcasm.

I was amused those four years had elapsed and their modern-day barn—the garage—was still overflowing with a surplus. I thought back to the pandemic period when we were overrunning the stores and emptying the shelves of every conceivable item we felt we'd need if the supply chains failed. Panic touched everyone to some degree. Nothing mattered except making sure we had enough of any and everything to help us survive a scourge that threatened our existence. It was a scary time. I imagine the comic strip couple were not the only ones guilty of "over preparing," essentially hoarding the "treasures" of the moment in hopes that by so doing, they would be saved from disaster.

A dive into scripture confirms that this human tendency to hoard, to store up so-called earthly treasures is nothing new. As noted in the chapter scriptures, the wisdom writer thousands of years ago cautioned against it, referring to it as a "grievous evil" that can bring harm to the owner. And the New Testament writer of Matthew's Gospel is just as clear. We are to not hoard or overstore earthly things as they too easily can become our treasures. It is impossible for the secular stuff we treasure not to affect our hearts, our souls; that part of us that belongs exclusively to God.

Some scholars suggest that hoarding is just another form of idolatry; the worship of something other than God as if it *were* God. Our first commandment from Him leaves no doubt that we who believe in Him are forbidden from putting anything before Him. The panic of the pandemic pushed many into just that. Hoarding became an obsession; an attempt to control what was beyond our control. And rather than trusting God with the pandemic "big picture," we felt the need to help Him out. That manifested in our storing up as much as we could while we could before the supplies ran out. Forget about what our neighbors lacked or could use. Forget about what our faith tells us about looking to the needs of others along with our own. So caught up in what I term the lure of lust, we forgot that God the creator of all things, who allowed the pandemic to blight the earth for reasons we may never understand, is still the provider of *all* things.

The comic strip is a reminder of the lesson Jesus taught us in the Gospel of Luke 12:12–21, NIV. Commonly known as the "Parable of the Rich Fool," it tells of a man rich with such an overabundance of crops that he had no room for the surplus and was forced to build bigger barns to house (hoard) all his grain and goods. When he had filled all the shelves with more than he would use, he declared he could take life easy. Jesus pronounced his actions those of a "fool," and concluded that he would not be around to enjoy those possessions. They would languish on the full shelves bringing no succor to him. He had invested in accumulating more than he needed; he was greedy and concerned with his own survival. Jesus ended His discourse with "This is how it will be with anyone who stores up things for himself (*or his family*–my insertion) but is not rich toward God." (Luke 12:21 NIV)

We, like our comic strip characters, if we're not on guard, slip easily into the mindset of hoarding. We don't think of it in that sense, so infatuated with the newest trends, or simply the sense that "I may need this one day," and of course that day seldom comes. Our shelves, closets, nooks, and crannies overflow with our material treasures. Let us be motivated one day soon to look up at these storage places, in our homes, garages or the storage units that have become the current "barns" for our hoarding or storing more than we need or will ever use.

And on a more serious note, may we also admit that often we hoard or store up in the "barn" we call our heart attitudes and feelings that displease God as does our overstoring of material things. Look inwardly. Are there stacks of pride, negative thinking, jealousy, anger, self-pity, lust, lackluster trust, or other behaviors that do not reflect the image of Christ there in this place reserved for Him? Hopefully, these moments of reflection when we do forces a reexamination of why we are hoarding an overflow of that which displeases God rather than being rich toward Him by releasing what doesn't belong in our heart and sharing with others our material excess. We don't know what our comic strip couple decided to do with their abundance of the four-year accumulation of toilet paper. But the humor inherent in it can translate into an opportunity to see and sense God in the most mundane. And perhaps to use that glimpse of Him as reason enough to grow more in obedience to and like Him.

Faith Footprint: At this writing, Spring is just a few days away. Whether it is or not when you read the chapter, think about doing an inventory of your storage haunts. Are there items unworn, unused that you know in your heart never will be? Pray about changing that trait to hoard or overstore and do a spring-cleaning that honors God and His blessing that allowed you to have all you do. And while you're at it, do the same for the debris residing in your heart. I know God will be pleased.

Chapter Twenty

Hoarding 102

*"When they had all had enough to eat, he said to his disciples,
"Gather the pieces that are left over. Let nothing be wasted.""*
~John 6:12 NIV

Today is the fifth Sunday of Lent, and I am on the computer. I never write on Sundays! It's a day for worship and rest, not work. Writing is my work—voluntary work, yes, but still work. What am I doing here? Answer: allowing God to reveal His divine presence in the ordinary once again. The ordinary was my sleeping, the gift of rest and revitalization He blesses us with at the culmination of a day. He came in a dream that suggested chapter nineteen was unfinished; that there was more to this "hoarding" concept to be revealed. His suggestions were hazy when I awakened, but the sense that He was speaking was not. I wished I had taken notes in that intimate moment of His Presence. As the morning unfolded, I settled down to my devotional time: reading His word and the words of others He has appointed to write of His goodness and grace as expressed in the Holy Word. The referenced scripture above prompted this chapter. It was as if He was saying to me, *"You didn't get it during my visit last night. Maybe this will help."* And it did.

In this miracle story of Jesus' feeding of the thousands with a child's lunch basket provisions, God speaks to our theme of the ungodliness of unnecessary storing—hoarding—of what He supplies. In its interpretation of what transpired during that seminal "food basket distribution," the devotional reminded me of what transpired. Upon accepting what they needed, the people had enough. There were no reports of folks trying to tuck extras into their pockets or hold onto the basket for themselves as it passed. They took what they needed; not what they thought they might need another day. Not even the leftovers were packed into individual to-go boxes. Rather, Jesus told the disciples to gather what was left so it would not be wasted.

Think of the implications for us today. We squirrel away more than we need in the moment for a future time we say we might need it. Too often than not that time never comes. When that happens, we resort to Plan B. Our modern day "barns" become the repositories of the surpluses that in time we forget about. Such solutions translate into wasteful practice. And Jesus said, "Let nothing be wasted." The scriptures do not reveal what happened to the uneaten food following the food distribution event on the mount. But I think we can surmise it didn't get thrown into barns to rot. In some form or fashion, it would have been shared in a moment with others in need. Perhaps a traveling food bank? Who knows? We can only speculate. But just the words of Christ regarding the extras give meaning to what we today should be doing regarding our tendency to overstore, to overspend, to overstock beyond our ability to use. To Hoard. It is a human tendency that denies our faith. We who profess Christ must learn and practice temperance, self-restraint, moderation, and self-control. No matter what the perceived threats of dwindling supplies of anything suggests, we live in faith that our God, the provider of everything will keep His promises. May the benefits of zero monthly storage fees, uncluttered cupboards and closets be the goal for which we strive as we mature more into the images of Jesus as scriptures reveal.

Faith Footprint: Clean out your refrigerators. Do you really need two of them—in the house and the garage? What about the freezer packed with food you never cook because it's there so long freezer burn makes it impossible to use? How many of the kitchen cupboards are occupied by expired staples? Is there food stuff you can donate to the local food banks? Perform an "Am I a Hoarder" test on yourself. Take intentional steps to change if it reveals that's what you are.

Footnote: I hold to my premise that God reveals His divine Presence in the most ordinary experiences of our living. Be on the alert for Him! He's where you least expect Him to be. What a joy!

Chapter Twenty-one

CALLER I.D.

"Call to me and I will answer you and tell you great and unsearchable things you do not know."

~Jeremiah 33:3 NIV

believe I've found my service niche in my new church home after a couple of misses. It falls under the umbrella of the church's prayer ministry with a unique twist I find refreshing and fulfilling. Referred to as the "After Care Call" ministry, its purpose is to stay connected to members of the congregation during and up to one year following the death of a family member. Monthly, I receive a list naming fifteen or more such members with their phone contact information. My task is simple. Place a "welfare" call to check in on how they're doing and offer support via prayer, words of encouragement, resources, or a listening ear. I've come to look forward to this outreach effort as it uplifts my spirit as much as I hope my efforts do for those with whom I speak.

Quickly, I learned that my call—ministry efforts would not be achieved as easily as phoning someone might imply. Though the technological advancements that enable the calls are a most efficient method of communicating, dialing the number does not guarantee a connection to the person you're attempting to reach. An "I.D." (identification) guardian answers when the prospective recipient's phone does not recognize the caller's identity. *"The person you are calling is not available. At the tone, please leave your message,"* is often than not what I hear, rather than a "Hello." My words are spoken not to the person on my list, but to their message mailbox.

Not one easily thwarted in my efforts, I've adapted a "script" so to speak of the message I would have spoken had my callee answered, but I admit it's not as inspirational as actual conversation. The best calls are the ones that connect and the person I'm calling answers the phone.

Recently, I thought about my ministry efforts when I read the chapter passage in Jeremiah. At the time God spoke to the prophet, Jeremiah was still in confinement in the courtyard of the guards. "Call me and I will answer..." God said. Jeremiah would not encounter in that effort to speak to God anyone blocking his call. Nowhere in scripture is there a suggestion that access to Him is controlled by a heavenly screening system. No Gabriel-like angel who supervises the call center section of Heaven; peering over the shoulders of operators who send calls either directly to God's private line or redirect them to His voice mail.

The Lord's directive to Jeremiah suggests to me that God wants to hear from us no matter where we are or what we're going through. All we must do is obey and call Him; not on a phone of course but using the system He set in place—prayer. Isn't that what prayer is after all? A call to the Master, our father in heaven, the Creator. I'm reminded of the lyrics of an old gospel song that reminds us God is always available whether we call Him in the morning, at midday, in the evening, or in the middle of the night. Are there "courtyards" in which you, like Jeremiah, are confined now? Perhaps a courtyard of depression, of health challenges, of financial woes, of loved ones struggling to live their faith? No matter the situation or the challenge, you can call Him. Even if all you want to do is share your joys of the moment or ask for strength to stay the course despite the temptation not to, you can call Him and He will answer. He recognizes our name when it appears on the line, and He will pick up. He delights in hearing from us, the sound of our voices. Take heart. God has cleared the way. He banished the I.D. and voicemail system an overzealous newbie angel thought was a perfect idea to manage the sheer volume of prayer calls that poured in to the Almighty. He learned quickly that God's ways were already perfect, as He is the epitome of perfection.

So, go ahead from whatever form of confinement you find yourself and call Him in prayer. He has promised to answer.

Faith Footprint: Think about your prayer practices. Do you only have set times to pray? Is prayer time slipshod, or can God count on hearing from you often to keep your relationship with Him alive and well? What needs tweaking, so that He isn't forced to get your attention in ways you may wish to avoid? Be deliberate and intentional. Pray. He's waiting. He will answer.

Chapter Twenty-two

SEEKER OR SETTLER?

"Seek the Lord while he may be found, call upon him while he is near..."

~Isaiah 55:6 NRSV

"With my whole heart I seek you; do not let me stray from your commandments."

~Psalms 119:10 NRSV

The King James Bible Dictionary, using as its source Webster's 1828 Dictionary, provides the following definition of the term seek: *"to go in search or quest of; to look for, to endeavor to find or gain by any means."* My thoughts turn to this season's Lenten study as it draws closer to Day 40 and its conclusion. This is Holy Week for Christians around the world. Since Ash Wednesday, we have tried to become more intentional in the exercise of our faith as witness to the significance of the upcoming pivotal moment of it. For almost forty days we have attempted through lingering in God's word to be poster children of the chapter verses.

We have discovered that "seeking" God is no passive endeavor, but rather one that requires a step out of the comfort zones that "Settlers" of the faith embrace. For many the first discovery was that the usual rote routines were insufficient. The quick, *"Thank you, Lord for a new day,"* as we embarked upon whatever the new day held had to be kicked up several notches if we were going to be serious about this lingering in God's Word, if we were to be instead "Seekers" of the Lord.

The forty-day study required not only reading the scriptures and the accompanying commentary, but also reflecting upon what we had read by journaling responses to specific questions. Those who thought their days of reading and writing had long since passed were jolted perhaps. What's this? You expect me to do more than just listen? You want me to fill in these spaces in the book with my thoughts and responses? The answer was "Yes," that's the expectation in this deeper dive into how we reflect the faith we profess.

Five days away now from Resurrection Sunday, the challenges of the selected scriptures have confirmed for some that they are on the right track; for some those same scriptures have forced reexamination of long-held beliefs and practices that deny they are seekers of the Lord; for others the daily study has both convicted and reassured them that there is yet hope for a turnaround, a restart, a clearer path than the one they'd settled for.

This time lingering in the word of God if nothing else has shone a light we cannot afford to ignore. If our goal is to obey God as an expression of our love of Him, then we must daily seek Him, His Face, His will; and with all the strength He gives us, we must resist faith practices that stamp us as "Settlers." We engage Him daily in scripture to heighten our understanding that settling is static. It's comfortable with the way things are, rather than as they can be when we gear up and seek the Lord with all we are, all we have.

Faith Footprint: Take some time and examine your faith practices. Are you one who intentionally spends significant time with God daily, seeking Him in every aspect of your Life?

Be honest. Off the top of your head, would you describe yourself as a "Seeker" or "Settler" of the Lord? If the latter, what corrective steps might you take to switch those?

Chapter Twenty-three

Swap Camera

"Do not judge, so that you may not be judged. For with the judgment you make you will be judged, and the measure you give will be the measure you get. Why do you see the speck in your neighbor's eye, but do not notice the log in your own eye? Or how can you say to your neighbor, 'Let me take the speck out of your eye,' while the log is in your own eye? You hypocrite, first take the log out of your own eye, and then you will see clearly to take the speck out of your neighbor's eye."

~Matthew 7:1–5 NRSV

*L*ittle did the designers of today's most ubiquitous gadget—the cell phone—know that one of its features would give opportunity for users to grab a glimpse of the Divine within the design element. *What, you say? God in an iPhone? Or its rival, an Android? Indeed,* I respond. The evidence is as follows.

The guest preacher from Vegas' sermon topic was "Loss Lives Matter." He offered several sermonic points to drive home that premise of his discourse. He was as we say of the "old school" gospel preaching model that was the gem of the African American Sunday morning worship experience. With wit and humor laced with authenticity and unwavering faith in the gospel of Jesus Christ, he touched the hearts and minds of those gathered in fellowship. Midway through the sermon, he pulled out his cell phone, held it up and began scanning the sanctuary; offering humorous commentary as the phone moved up and down, side to side: *"I see you brother up there falling asleep. You were out late last night, huh? And you, sister, you're sending text messages while I'm preaching, right?"* Laughter filled the pews as you might imagine. Then, turning his attention to the phone, he pointed out that when he held it in that position, he could see what everybody else was up to, but if he tapped the icon beneath that read "Swap Camera," the image reversed and what he saw was himself. His perspective had changed. No longer could he point to what they were doing or not doing, for staring back was not *them*, but *him*, his own reflection. His cell phone demo made the point. When our focus is on other folks and their shortcomings, we forget the message of the chapter verses.

In 1988, the reigning icon of pop music, Michael Jackson, released a song that topped the billboards, becoming his tenth number one single hit song. The choral lyrics of *"Man in the Mirror"* capture the essence of the pastor's cell phone sermonic point.

Look at yourself first; before you pass judgement, re-adjust your perspective. Such self-reflection forces confession and admittance that you are saved not by your exterior persona, what you preen over gazing at your hot self. No, you and we, are saved by God's grace who sees the real us beneath the image reflected on the screen. He sees where it matters, into our hearts.

Now, who would think that this pervasive, ever present communication tool could illuminate the presence of the Divine in such a way. Yes, we use it for reference to His word with our Bible apps and other devotional aides; but to expand our sense of Him where we least expect—the camera and its features—is a definite "Aha." In my mind anyway.

Faith Footprint: If faultfinding or criticism is second nature to you, take definite steps to curb this behavior Jesus so clearly speaks to in the chapter verses. Put it on your personal prayer list as something to work on with the help of the Holy Spirit every day. Keep a record of your wins and losses as inspiration to make the change.

Chapter Twenty-four

PUFF. PUFF. PASS.

"Sing to all the earth. Tell of his salvation from day to day. Declare his glory among the nations, his marvelous works among all the people."

~1 Chronicles 16:23–24 NRSV

"Go therefore and make disciples of all nations, … teaching them everything I have commanded you."

~Matthew 28:19–20 NRSV

"But how are they to call on one in whom they have not believed? And how are they to believe in one of whom they have never heard? And how are they to hear without someone to proclaim him? And how are they to proclaim him unless they are sent? As it is written, 'How beautiful are the feet of those who bring good news.'"

~Romans 10:14–15 NRSV

"So, we are ambassadors for Christ, … "

~2 Corinthians 5:20 NRSV

"I solemnly urge you: proclaim the message; be persistent whether the time is favorable or unfavorable; convince, rebuke, and encourage, with the utmost patience in teaching."

~2 Timothy 4:1–2 NRSV

Consider this chapter if you will, a follow up to the preceding one. The setting remains the same: Sunday morning worship with the sermon title, "*Loss Lives Matter.*" As the guest pastor assured us, he was almost done (a commonly uttered pastoral statement that seldom manifests), he shared a memory of himself as a youth engaged with his compadres in a forbidden, but common activity of his era. From his telling, at an appointed time, he and his "besties" would gather in a circle behind the gym area. There they would share the thrill and high of smoking a single joint of weed. That's right. One joint for the eight of them. The rule of the circle he explained was simple. As the joint passed, they could take only two puffs; then they had to pass the highly treasured commodity to the next person. The underlying wisdom of the ritual was simple: the euphoric feeling of the puffs must be shared. No keeping for just oneself what brought such joy. And the only way to ensure that all knew that joy was to follow the rule and pass it on. Then in that way common to gifted ministers of the Gospel, he told us the circle rule was called, "Puff, puff. Pass."

The congregation exploded in laughter. I admit I was somewhat bewildered. I'd never heard the phrase, and it seemed I was in the minority, as most apparently had. (As a member of the over sixty demographic in a congregation tilted to the under fifty crowd, I wasn't surprised) As the hilarity eventually faded, the pastor linked those youthful moments of indiscretion (before he was obviously saved and sanctified), to his theme. If lost lives matter, we as Christ followers have a responsibility to those who fall into the category of "lostness." From the Old Testament proclamation in Chronicles to Jesus' commission in the Gospel of Matthew and continuing throughout the New Testament, the apostles and disciples shared what they held priceless.

We are called to do the same. We must intentionally share what we value, our spiritual commodity, our faith, the grace God extends to us. Keeping for ourselves the gift of grace He has given was never His intent. In all the details of our living, the rule of the circle must prevail. Too many "lost lives" are dependent upon us to pass the faith. We need not worry that there isn't enough, or we'll run out of it. As did those young delinquents behind the gym with their marijuana joint, we Christ followers today can unselfishly "puff, puff, pass" God's "joint" of grace in hope that by our actions and within the details of our living we will point others toward Him. Expand the circle, and its rules of sharing. The faith "joint" need not be hidden, nor for the few.

Once again within what on the surface might appear a simple cultural phenomenon, we see the extraordinary twist of the Divine within, offering us yet another sense of His sovereignty in all things.

Faith Footprint: Reflect upon ways you might better be a sharer of the Good News, as opposed to someone content with enjoying your joys and blessings as treasures just for yourself.

Chapter Twenty-five

LOVE IS IN THE DETAILS

"Love is patient, love is kind. It does not envy, it does not boast, it is not proud. It is not rude, it is not self-seeking, it is not easily angered, it keeps no record of wrongdoing. Love does not delight in evil but rejoices with the truth. It always protects, always trusts, always hopes, always perseveres."

~1 Corinthians 13:4–7 NIV

"For God so loved the world that he gave his one and only son…"

~John 3:16 NIV

"But God demonstrates his own love for us in this: While we were still sinners, Christ died for us.

~ Romans 5:8 NIV

"But the fruit of the Spirit is love. …"

~Galatians 5:22 NIV

"If you really keep the royal law found on Scripture, Love your neighbor as yourself, you are doing right."

~James 2:8 NIV

"Do not love the world or anything in the world. If anyone loves the world the love of the Father is not in him."

~1 John 2:15 NV

"Let us not love with words or tongue, but with actions and in truth."

~1 John 3:18 NIV

"Love the Lord your God with all your heart and with all soul and with all your mind. ... Love your neighbor as yourself. All the Law and the Prophets hang on these two commandments."
~Matthews 22:37–40 NIV

The Purina cat food advertisement caught my eye. I don't know why, as no one would ever refer to me as a cat lover. They're too quiet for my taste. If you got to have an animal companion, a dog in my opinion is a better choice. But for some reason, I paused and stared at the domestic scene of the human preparing her cat's meal, scooping the concoction into a crystal bowl, a smile on her face as she offered provisions for it. Obviously accustomed to such adoration, the fluffy white feline sat quietly in the frame waiting to have its needs met by its human caregiver. I glanced again at the ad's title: *"Love is in the details."*

Catchy, I thought, and a whimsical way to suggest that it is in the things a pet owner willingly does for its four-legged friend that said owner demonstrates her/his affection for it. The subliminal messaging makes the point—loving reveals itself in the everyday rhythms of living, what we do and how we do it reflecting its authenticity in the basics and beyond.

The leap from that thought to *"Kinda like how God manifests His love for us and in turn we demonstrate ours for Him,"* wasn't long in coming. Once again within the mundane the Lord's exhibition of His divinity burst through. Consider the following:

- We belong to God, our Creator. Because we are His, He takes seriously our well-being. He provides for our daily and long-term needs for shelter and sustenance as does the owner of the cat in the advertisement.
- He searches for us when we lose our way and can't find the path home to Him as does the cat owner who posts the "Lost Cat" flyers around the community seeking its safe return.
- Our names are written in the palm of His hand as proof of ownership, as the kitty's collar reveals to whom it belongs.
- When we slip and fall into the mire of temptation and sinful

choices, He lifts us up and out, cleanses us of that which is displeasing and dishonoring of Him as does the pet owner when kitty comes home covered in the dirt and filth it has picked up in the alleyways it traverses.

- Though we often disappoint Him in our waywardness and backsliding, He cares for us anyway as His faithfulness never ends.

And on the flip side of that "love coin," our love for God is manifested not just by our simple utterance, "*I love the Lord.*" It must reveal itself in our actions and attitudes. Scripture is clear in what that looks like:

- Jesus speaks in John 14:15—"*If you love me, you will obey what I have commanded.*"
- The Apostle John declares in 1 John 5:3—"*This is love for God: to obey his commands.*"

Obedience to the God to whom we profess to belong is the best way to demonstrate our love for Him. Is there an artist in the house to capture that visual?

Faith Footprint: Make a list of the ways you daily and intentionally manifest your love of God. If you're the creative type, draw a picture of what that looks like.

An Interlude

*T*oday is April 8, 2024, and I decided to pause midway through this latest book to reflect upon the mania and frenzy that a total solar eclipse has produced leading up to it. In bold font, yesterday's newspaper banner headline read **Chasing the majesty** to describe what has captivated North Americans from Mexico to Canada and across the contiguous United States. The eclipse is the first one over the US since 2017, with the next one not predicted to appear until 2033. In the areas of North America where darkness will reign for a short period of time as the moon completely blocks the light of the sun, crowds have converged, eager to gaze upon the wonder of such heavenly 'majesty.' Even the electronic freeway and highway signs signal its coming by advising drivers to "expect delays, leave early, stay in place, and plan to leave late." Without doubt, it has garnered as much if not more attention than the current wars in Europe, the Middle East, and the nation of Haiti. At least for one day!

The eagerly anticipated celestial wonder's impact revised teacher lesson plans, was projected to boost the economy in the areas over which it would cross, increase road traffic, affect air travel, and prompt a surge in hotel occupancy. The 24–7 media hype leading up to the day cast a spell that was difficult to resist. Indeed, it seemed everybody was caught up in *"chasing the majesty"* of such a display of power and splendor.

I'm probably in the minority among those who read more into the eclipse headline than perhaps what was intended by the newspaper. I confess my initial reaction to the term 'majesty' (notably sans capitalization) within the heavenly realm is that of His Majesty, the God who created the universe and all therein, including eclipses. Chasing that Majesty is an understandable pursuit. But equating an eclipse with the only entity I believe to be Majestic and chasing it across the nation—that I don't get.

As I'm writing now the eclipse has moved on. For several minutes as it passed my area, the sky darkened to such an extent that my outdoor security lights came on as if it were nighttime. I sat quietly waiting to return to the keyboard. In a reflective mood, I pondered how easily seduced the populace had been by this natural wonder. Nothing mattered except being in its path, marveling at its awesomeness, being able to say, "I *saw it for myself*." And coming away with a sense of having been touched by something beyond natural, something more grandeur than the humdrum of daily living.

I wondered how different the world might be if we exhibited that level of fervor and enthusiasm to espy the Creator of today's eclipse and all the other wonders of the solar system. If we dropped everything, spared no expense, and incorporated even the mundane into pursuing Him as so many have done for the months, weeks and days leading up to today. What might happen if we set aside more of the routines that govern our activities; if we were willing to wait on our Majestic God to show up in His timing to turn the darknesses of our situations into the light of His will; if we refused to allow another twenty-four hours to pass without incorporating a significant amount of it soaking in His Word and learning from the wonder it reveals?

As I may have mentioned at some point, I jot ideas in a small notebook titled, *A Writer is a Dreamer*. I own that sense of word crafting, putting into words the dreams that are forever unfolding. It is perhaps that sense of dreaming that it is possible still for us, God's human creation, to shift from chasing that which is awe-inspiring yet temporary to chasing the Creator of all that is lasting and eternal which keeps me on the alert for His Presence.

I imagine Him waiting today for that one awakened soul to get it; to shift his/her focus from the darkness of an eclipse to light of His love; to recall words of the book of Genesis: "In the beginning God created the heaven and the earth. ... And God said, 'Let there be light.' ... God made two great lights—the greater light to govern the day and the lesser light to govern the night." And in that recalling of how the story began look up in awe toward the One who created all.

Perhaps that one awakened person is you. For within the uniqueness of a solar eclipse, God is surely present.

"O Lord, our Lord, how majestic is your name in all the earth."
~Psalm 8:1 NIV

"For great is the Lord and most worthy of praise; ... splendor and majesty are before him; strength and joy in his dwelling place. ... Ascribe to the Lord, O families of earth, ascribe to the Lord the glory due his name."
~1 Chronicles 16:25–28 NIV

"Yours, O Lord, is the greatness and the power and the glory and the majesty and the splendor, for everything in heaven and earth is yours."
~1 Chronicles 29:11 NIV

"We did not follow cleverly invented stories when we told you about the power and coming of our Lord Jesus Christ, but we were eyewitnesses of his majesty. For he received honor and glory from God the Father when the voice came to him from the Majestic Glory, saying, 'This is my Son, whom I love; with him I am well pleased."
~2 Peter 1:16–17 NIV

Chapter Twenty-six

SETTLER OR SEEKER—PART TWO

"But if from there you seek the Lord your God, you will find him if you seek him with all you heart and with all your soul."
~Deuteronomy 4:29 NIV

"Seek the Lord while he may be found; call on call on him while his is near."
~Isaiah 55:6 NIV

"For I know the plans I have for you, declares the Lord. ... you will seek me and find me when you seek me with all your heart."
~Jeremiah 29:11, 13 NIV

"But seek first his kingdom and his righteousness, and all these things will be given to you as well."
~Matthew 6:33 NIV

"From one man he made every nation of men, that they should inhabit the whole earth; and he determined the times set for them and the exact places where they should live. God did this so that men would seek him and perhaps reach out to him and find him, though he is not far from each one of us."
~Acts 17:26–27 NIV

Four chapters prior (# 22) I explored some concepts of what it means to be a "seeker" of God as opposed to a "settler" in terms of one's faith. The intent of this chapter is to delve more into the significance of the terms for those who profess Jesus as Christ and are trying to live in ways that confirm their faith. With that as our assumption, let's see if within the scriptures we discern God is more likely to be found in one trait rather than the other.

The word settler commonly refers to someone who moves to a new country or place to begin a new life. It sometimes also describes a person who "settles" for something or someone who may or may not be what he/she really desires. The individual "makes do" with what he has or where he is. A "seeker" on the other hand is a searcher, someone who is in pursuit of something, something more than what they now have; something worth searching for.

The scriptural reference from the Book of Acts sets the backdrop for the concept of settling. God seems to imply that we are created to settle down and within that space turn our attention to pursuing Him. That concept is as true for us as it was for our biblical forefathers. We allow His Spirit to lead us to a community of faith with whom we can settle as the body of Christ. And that's what most of us do. Whether it's the church home in which we grew up or one we find on our own, we respond to the invitation and settle in. In our pew, in our Bible study class, the choir, the usher board, the various volunteer opportunities, we settle down. We've checked all the boxes, dotted the i's, and crossed the t's. We are comfortable wearing the Faith Settler brand, content to "rest on our laurels," seemingly unaware of the abundant life Christ promises.

Perhaps there is nothing inherently wrong with sporting that brand, but scriptures do suggest there is more to be had, if we are to know the fullness of God's grace. We are advised to seek the Lord while He may be found, suggesting that a time will come when that opportunity may not be available. Furthermore, we are admonished to seek Him with our heart and soul, to seek His kingdom and His righteousness, because He has plans for our lives that will come to fruition only when we do. Seeking as I've noted above implies doing something, of being on the hunt, in constant pursuit of the God we worship. We come to realize that our faith profession should be in constant motion; beyond Sunday services, we read and study to know the Lord more fully. We spend dedicated quiet time in His Presence. We pray unceasingly. We use the disciplines of our faith profession to keep us alert to opportunities to search for Him in everything—the good, bad, the ugly. As the psalmist instructs us, we:

> *"Look to the Lord and his strength; seek his face always."*
> ~Psalm 105:4 NIV

Settling, in my opinion, does just the opposite. It denies the wonders and possibilities of God's hand in the mundane as well as the divine occurrences in life. Why be a settler? Choose instead the exhilaration of being a seeker and enjoy the added plus—those sporting the Faith Seeker brand stand out in the crowd! Their joy in the Lord is contagious!

Faith Footprint: What are you? A settler of seeker of the faith? If you've abandoned the "seeker" traits of your faith, what can you do to rekindle it?

Chapter Twenty-seven

Just Across the Street

"He who dwells in the shelter of the Most High will rest in the shadow of the Almighty. I will say of the Lord, he is my refuge and my fortress, my God in whom I trust."

~Psalm 91:1–2 NIV

"One thing I ask of the Lord, this is what I seek; that I may dwell in the house of the Lord all the days of my life, to gaze upon the beauty of the Lord and to seek him in his temple."

~Psalm 27:4–5 NIV

"We wait in hope for the Lord; he is our help and our shield. In him our heats rejoice, for we trust in his holy name."

~Psalm 33:20–22 NIV

A couple of weeks ago I flew to Decatur, Georgia, to spend a week with my son who had been admitted to a long-term acute care hospital following a three-week stint in an ICU ward for treatment of a lung malfunction. The severity of his condition resulted in him requiring a ventilator to breathe. The acute care hospital admitted patients who needed specialized treatment to restore independent breathing sans ventilators and trach collars.

My visit was two-fold in purpose: to be physically present with him as he adjusted to his new environment, offering motherly comfort, assurance, and encouragement; and as importantly to put a face to the voice of the mom who would be calling several times a day for staff updates on the progress of her Sonshine. It was daunting to say the least to see the multiple machines required to monitor everything connected to keeping him alive and breathing. Yet despite what I espied from that perspective, it was a joy to note that the spark of life which emanated from his countenance remained. His silent acknowledgement of my presence with a nod of his head confirmed it was good that I was there with him.

What was to be an eight-day visit had been cut short one day because of the impact of the 2024 total solar eclipse on air travel. The airline cancelled and rebooked flights; and by God's grace I located a hotel only six minutes away from the hospital. We settled easily into our morning to early evening time together. I read both scriptures and devotionals. He listened via headphones to his gospel music playlists. He's watched his favorite TV soap, *Greenleaf*, on my iPad. And interspersed with those activities, his therapists put him through his paces. Most importantly, we were together; the silence as much a blessing as everything else that consumed our time.

As I recall, it was the second day I signed in at the desk when the receptionist told me the hospital validated parking if I parked in their lot, but parking was free across the street in the church's parking lot during the weekdays. The next morning as I turned the corner, I noticed the lot to which she referred and glanced upward. The huge lot abutted the sanctuary and adjacent buildings of the Decatur United Methodist Church. I was astounded. A United Methodist Church set across the street from Emory Long Term Acute Care Hospital. No way was that a coincidence! No way. When I arrived at Quentin's room, I blurted, "Sonshine, guess what's across the street from here. A United Methodist Church! How awesome is that!" He nodded. The staff person who happened to be in his room looked at me inquiringly, and I explained we were life-long United Methodists, that as a child he had been baptized and at age twelve confirmed in that denomination. To have that church situated there had to be divinely ordained!

For the remainder of my visit, simply looking out the window of the room at the church buildings, the tall stately steeple gave me a sense of peace, of God's Presence. Though I had no opportunity to worship in its sanctuary, just the knowledge that the presence of the

Lord was that physically close to my "grown-man baby" somehow boosted my spirits.

During his nap times, I walked the corridors of his floor to get as many of my daily steps in as possible. It also gave me time for reflection allowing me to "be still before the Lord and wait patiently for him" (Psalm 37:7 NIV); and to recall "God is my refuge and strength, an ever-present help in trouble." (Psalm 46:1 NIV) Upon returning to his room, the dominant visual remained. The body of Christ as represented by His church stood guard, so to speak; just another reminder to me that His plans for my son, my Sonshine rest in His hands, His timing. Just "across the street."

Faith Footprint: In one of your dedicated quiet times with the Lord, reflect upon something manmade that has served or still serves as a visual reminder to you of Him being your refuge and strength, especially as you wait for prayers to be answered.

Chapter Twenty-eight

It's the Little Things

$\mathscr{R}$ecently I watched a Denzel Washington movie released in 2021 that though a longtime fan I am had somehow missed. Titled *The Little Things*, he portrays a veteran sheriff who joins forces with a rookie officer to track down a serial killer terrorizing Los Angeles. As the iconic actor has aged, so have the roles he plays. They mirror his longevity; his characters are often cast as sages. At a pivotal point in the hunt to prove their prime suspect is the responsible party, Denzel says to the young sergeant, "*It's the little things that get you caught,*" implying that the suspected killer will more than likely be apprehended by some little thing he does. That line stuck.

I've mulled it over several weeks now and realize it's less the ambiguity of the movie's ending that causes that line to cling to my consciousness and more a sense that often the little things in life can do more than trap you. They can also shed light on who we are; and as importantly, illuminate our faith. Both the Gospels of Mark and Luke offer examples of life's little gestures or expressions that highlight just that. When Jesus encountered a man with a shriveled hand, he said to him, "Stretch out your hand." The man stretched it out and his hand was healed. (Mark 3:1–5 NIV) A woman in the crowd who had suffered from bleeding for twelve years followed Him on His way to heal a synagogue leader's daughter. When she was close enough to touch the hem of His garment, she did so because as scripture records, she thought, "If I just touch his clothes, I will be healed." (Mark 5:25-28 NIV) And at yet another time when thousands gathered to hear Him teach without access to food, Jesus told the disciples to feed them. With two loaves of bread and five fish offered by a young boy, they not only fed them, but collected twelve baskets of leftovers. (Mark 6:35–44 NIV) "But say the word and my servant will be healed," the centurion said to Jesus. He believed in Jesus' power to do so without even being in the servant's presence. Jesus was amazed at this faith expression such that He exclaimed, "I tell you I have not found such great faith even in Israel." (Luke 7:1–9 NIV) Each occurrence could be termed a little thing, yet each had profound consequences.

Though we too often are prone to relegate these stories to the times of our biblical ancestors and not to the times in which we live, nonetheless they give witness to my assertion. The little things we do today tell our story as it did theirs. Within them God moves if we allow Him and reminds us He is in everything.

Those little things: reflected in our actions, our speech, our thinking, speak volumes. A blind eye turned to the person seeking help. The tone of voice used to respond to that person who gets on your last nerve. The "silent" treatment given to your spouse when conflict remains unresolved. The decision to buy yet another pair of shoes, another handbag, another anything that you already have more of than you use. That donation box you said you'd fill with the stuff you've hoarded for so long. The things you keep putting off that you know need your attention. The spiritual disciplines of quiet time with the Lord daily, engaged in His word as eagerly as you are in watching your daily morning, afternoon, and evening television shows, or scrolling Facebook and other social media sites. The phone calls to family and friends just to say, "*Hi, I love you. Need anything?*" The friendly smile in the checkout line. Remembering, "Do to others what you would have them do to you." (Luke 6:31 NIV) The confidence at the doctor's appointment, even if the news is not what you'd hope to hear, that God's will is perfect and for your good and His glory.

Little things. They count. They reveal who we are because they reveal what's in our heart. And is it not there—the heart—where God looks? (1 Samuel 16:7 NIV)

Faith Footprint: Take time today to reflect upon the little things in your life that tell your story, that reflect your faith. If you have a hard time doing that, what might that say about your faith journey?

Chapter Twenty-Nine

"Meet Me at the Bench"

"Then Moses went up to God, and the Lord called to him from the mountain…"
~Exodus 19:3 NIV

"There he went into a cave and spent the night. And the word of the Lord came to him: 'What are you doing here, Elijah?'"
~1 Kings19:9 NIV

"As he neared Damascus on his journey, suddenly a light from heaven flashed around him. He fell to the ground and heard a voice say to him, 'Saul, Saul, why do you persecute me?'"
~Acts 9:3-4 NIV

*L*et me set the record straight before I begin. Today's chapter title is in italicized quotation marks because it jumped onto the page as soon as I read it in a morning's devotional. Quite literally, it nudged the chapter I'd begun for twenty-nine off the page. In the reading, a friend had spoken the phrase to the writer in reference to a bench in front of her house that had become a meet-up place for a multitude of reasons; and segued into her theme of having a place to regularly meet with Jesus. I immediately glanced down at my bedroom love seat upon which I was sitting and thought, *"That's where I am now, on my bench, my 'love' bench, meeting with my Savior."*

I drifted in thought to years past when the love seat in the office of my former home had served the same purpose: my meet-up bench for morning prayers, devotional and prayer line time; made even more precious and joyous by the presence of my youngest grandson, a toddler at the time, who faithfully crawled up to sit next to me as long as I was there. As the chapter verses so illustrate, this idea of meeting up with God is nothing new. He met Moses on a mountain. Elijah was hiding out in a cave when God met with him; and perhaps in the most startling example of one of His meetings, He accosted Saul on the road to Damascus to hold a meeting with him and discuss the error of his ways.

I am in complete agreement with the devotional writer who suggests we all need a place where we can have a little talk with the Lord; a quiet time in His Presence to offer praise and thanksgiving; and most importantly to be still and listen to His wisdom so that we can live daily in obedience to His teachings. Ever sensitive to our human frailties, He doesn't ask us to climb a mountain, seek solitude in a cave, or bring us to our knees with a blinding light on a local sidewalk to meet up with Him. He allows us to choose the spot. A patio bench, a sequestered garden nook, a closed-door closet, or simply our favorite chair. Wherever we choose, He will meet us there; eager to engage us in the highlights of the day, the prayers we lift, the sorrows and joys common to our human experience. On our "meet up bench," the Savior is there. Anytime—morning, noon, or night. Don't keep Him waiting.

Faith Footprint: Do you have a "*Meet up bench*," the place where you go to chat with the Lord? If you don't, think about choosing such a spot and see if it doesn't make a difference in your spiritual life.

Chapter Thirty

IMAGINE THAT!

For a week now one of my favorite comic strips has provided both my morning chuckle, the daily dose of humor which feeds my spirit as my various vitamins and supplements nourish my body, and a heightened sensitivity to the nuance of God's presence. In the strip's opening panel, the astonished mother with hands held to the sides of her head exclaims in astonishment the chapter's title as her teenage son voices his latest revelations with his peers. In each he proudly shares a piece of advice, i.e.

- *"I've noticed that the more sleep I get, the less I feel tired."*
- *"My room seems a lot less cluttered when I put things away."*
- *"I've discovered that there's actually less pressure when I don't put assignments off until the last minute."*

and other such wonderments. The humor flows from his sense that he's made a life discovery on his own, and the visual of the mother's expression that screams, *"How many times have I told him that; and now he thinks it's his idea, some new insight he's pulled out of thin air? Has he completely forgotten my efforts to get him to teach him just that?"* Anyone who's parented a teenager gets it. You wear yourself out teaching life lessons to help them mature responsibly. And in those moments the comic strip captures, the incredulity of what issues from their mouths blows you away.

As my purpose is to spot the Savior where least expected, the comic made me think of that biblical passage in the concluding chapter of the Gospel of Luke. In many Bibles it is subtitled, *"On the Road to Emmaus."* The text shares the conversation of two of Jesus' disciples walking along the road to the town of Emmaus following Jesus' crucifixion. Jesus (whose identity is unrevealed to them initially) joins them and asks what they're talking about. Thus follows their revelations about who Jesus was, what happened to Him and the surprising empty tomb where He had been buried. Verse 25 captures Jesus' seeming astonishment as He said to them, *"How foolish you are, and slow of heart to believe all that the prophets have spoken!"* I'm sure words along that line were burning on the tongue of the mom in the comic strip. Both she and the Savior marveled at the slowness of the ones they've taught to receive their message.

I don't see that much has changed. God has given us His word as revealed in our Bibles all we need to know to live life more fully and satisfactorily; in ways that acknowledge His sovereignty and bring Him glory. There is no excuse for doubts.

> *"He has shown you, O man, what is good. And what does the Lord require of you? To act justly and to love to mercy and to walk humbly with your God."*
>
> ~Micah 6:8 NIV

We may not have voiced as our comic strip character the words of our parents as personal insight, devoid of their wisdom, but our own. But many of us can confess we've tried to upend God's wisdom with our own versions of what He meant. We tweak it to fit our purposes, our plans. It's in those moments I image Him, hands held to His divine head, as speechless as the mom of a teen.

Faith Footprint: Reflect upon God's word. Do you find yourself thinking you already know its insights? That it's not news to you? That you've figured it out on your own? Is there danger in such an attitude for the believer? What might that be?

Chapter Thirty-one

WHERE YOU'RE SUPPOSED TO BE

"For I know the plans I have for you,' declares the Lord, 'plans to prosper you and not to harm you, plans to give you hope and a future."

~Jeremiah 29:11 NIV

*R*ecently as I watched the *Equalizer 3* movie for the third time, an exchange between the main character and the local doctor who had treated him for a gunshot wound stuck in my subconscious. In the role of a former CIA operative gone rogue who pursues justice for someone who's been wronged, he lies in bed in the doctor's home following the surgery that saved his life. Having no memory of how he'd gotten there, he asked, *"Where am I?"* The doctor replied, *"You're where you're supposed to be."*

As the movie unfolds, that simple statement takes on a deeper meaning; and Robert, aka Roberto, embraces it as he adjusts to the rhythms and customs of the small Italian village, becoming accepted by its residents as one of them, and reciprocating that bonding; sensing he is indeed where he's supposed to be. His transformation from a wandering righter of wrongs to a settling member of a community sets the continuing framework of the movie. And as expected, draws him back into his role of being an "equalizer." In the movie's defining moment, as he refuses to leave his fellow citizens to the vengeance of the bad guys, he declares he's not leaving this place where he has found peace and acceptance because, he's come to understand that *"this is where I'm supposed to be."*

I've concluded that life often mirrors his realization. Circumstances and challenges we did not expect can place us where we had not planned to be. I think back to the time before my son's unexpected stroke, and its ensuing aftermaths. That one of them would be my return to the place of my birth and maturation was not on my radar. To be honest, the negative feelings I'd harbored for this city since 1963 lingered in my subconscious. And though most of my maternal family members lived here, I'd ceased years ago to feel it was "home." That descriptor was reserved for the place I'd escaped to and lived in for most of my adult life. Yet here I am. And in the close to four years of my living in this quaint, quiet, serene area I'd never heard of back in the day, I can echo, "*This is where I'm supposed to be.*" The only negative is the distance created by my move between my son and my grandchildren, the "Grand Four."

I venture to say mine is not an uncommon experience. Both personal and professional circumstances often dictate changes in our life journey. Because we are not privy to the Lord's ultimate plans for us before He reveals them, we may find ourselves at that moment where we look around and ask, "*Where am I? What happened? How did I get here?*" I've decided these are moments I call "faith moments." The moments when we trust that irrespective of what it looks like, God knows what He's doing; that our confusion about how we got where we are, or why He even allowed us to venture into it in the first place give way to a realization of His promise being fulfilled. Though everything may not be exactly what we want or hoped for, and adjustments may be required to fit our desires into His purposes, and this new place may take some getting used to, it is where at this moment in our lives we are supposed to be. Why? Because God will be God and His plans for us will prevail.

God does His best work in and through us when we accept where He has placed us. His joy and peace abide there in the situations and challenges where we're supposed to be.

Faith Footprint: Are you presently in a place you'd rather not be? Is it possible that God has you there for His reasons? Pray for wisdom to discern if this is where He would have you be or one of your own choosing.

Chapter Thirty-two

BIRD BATTLE

"Look at the birds of the air; they do not sow or reap or stow away in barns, and yet your heavenly Father feeds them. Are you not much more valuable than they?"

~Matthew 6:26 NIV

Let me begin by acknowledging that birds are mentioned multiple times in both the Old and New Testaments. They symbolize God's provisionary concern for even the least of His creations. In the branches of trees, barns, and a host of other places, they find shelter, and places to nest. That's all well and good. This, however, is a saga of one of their more unsavory traits that is seldom mentioned in polite company but became for me anyway an annoyance that could not be ignored. I am still coming to terms with my months-long skirmishes with these God-created creatures that assumed gargantuan powers to frustrate my efforts to prevent them from nesting in the eaves of my roof and porch arches.

On the surface their nesting efforts would appear harmless. The reality is quite different. Those efforts to construct nests also produce nasty bird droppings on windows, doors, porches and entryway steps that are unsightly and unhealthy. As my glass entry door and the windows of the porch area beneath the eaves grew more and more smeared with what these little creatures produced and left behind, it became apparent that I had to respond. And so began the battle: the birds in one corner; Beverly in the other.

Understand. I wasn't attempting to deprive God's creatures of His provisions. That He was still feeding them was evident! What

I wanted was for them to find a place to build their nest away from human occupancy. I tried all the bird deterrents on the worldwide shopping site that will go unnamed. I learned that birds are afraid of owls so I placed two in the alcoves of the entry. That worked only for the short period it took them to figure out the owls weren't real. They returned to their flying in and out of said areas, leaving them as aforementioned. Using my water hose as my weapon of choice, I washed down the muddy grass they were using to build their nest. In a couple of days, they would start a new construction. For weeks, the battle went back and forth, each of us determined to undermine the other. Their tenacity would have been inspiring under different circumstances. Over the course of the ensuing rounds, I bought and returned a large battery-operated owl with flashing red eyes whose head swiveled as it made owl noises and a needle-like pin contraption that they ignored. Exhausted with the clean-ups and failing solutions, I dragged myself back into the ring one final time—fortified with an electronic bird deterrent sonar box and some commercial spikes used by companies to keep the creatures away. Finally, the little critters threw in the towel. I won. Where they went, I don't know. But they're gone.

As the weeks have passed (with my sonar box and spikes still in place), I've thought about this experience and wondered as I am prone to do what lesson the Lord might want me take away from it. It may be a stretch, but I think perhaps He's shown me that despite my efforts to thwart the birds' efforts to continue their purpose for being, they will do what they were created to do. God will provide both food and shelter for their nestlings, if not at my house, somewhere else. He will not abandon them. They will find fulfillment in His purposes.

It's a powerful lesson for me as well. As I struggled to prevent the birds roosting and the effects thereof, and eventually finding a solution that worked, God will provide for me in my efforts to confront the challenges life will continue to present. I may be blocked or delayed or stymied, but eventually with God as my provider and sustainer, I will prevail. No manmade plans or devises will thwart His purposes for my life.

Faith Footprint: Reflect upon a current challenge that is demanding a spirit of steadfastness. How is God helping you to stay the course?

Chapter Thirty-three

CONNECTIONS

"Here I am. I stand at the door and knock. If anyone hears my voice and opens the door, I will come in…"

~Revelations 3:20 NIV

*A*s you are familiar now with my underlying theme of showcasing the Lord in the common and ordinary things of my life, you'll get (I hope) why a *Zits* comic strip caught my attention. In the first frame, the mother asks her teenage son if there is *"Anything"* she can do to encourage him to talk to her, and he replies, *"Sure."* Slouching away with hands in pocket, he says, *"Just rap the entire soundtrack of Spider-Man into the Spider-Verse for me."* In the third and last frame he sits next to his dad with an expression of utter disbelief and says, *"And then she did it!"* To which dad nonchalantly replies, *"Never underestimate a mother's need for connection."*

Having parented a son, I identified with the mom. In the comic strips leading to this one, she had attempted to converse with him about any number of things—school, friends, activities, his feelings—with those efforts being brushed away with the classic teen eye-rolling or the one-word responses: *"yeah," "fine," "okay," "nothing."* While dads don't seem to have inherited this gene of a need to connect, mothers more than compensate for their laisse-faire spirit. Mom's DNA searches constantly for a way in, a way to help, a way to enhance her child's qualities and gifts, to not overlook any opportunity to steer him, her or them, toward the best possible future.

As I sat smiling at the memory reel running through my mind of those years when Quentin was in the throes of "teenagery" (my play on the word), I thought of our heavenly Father. Is He not the consummate example of a parent wanting, needing connection to/ with His offspring? An earthly mother's need comes nowhere near God's desire to connect with those He created. From the moment of our conception in the womb until He breathes life into our lungs at birth, God seeks us. He wants a connection with us from that moment onward.

His words confirm His desire, His need for us to stay connected. The wisdom writer of Proverbs reminds us in chapter 3, verses 5–6 (NIV), that if we trust God with our hearts and minds, lean not to our own understanding, and acknowledge Him in everything, He will provide guidance and right direction. Such a relationship ensures connection, which is what He wants. The prophet Isaiah (30:18 NIV) writes that "*the Lord longs to be gracious to you; he rises to show you compassion.*" God's word came to Jeremiah, and he recorded them in chapter 24, verse 7 (NIV): "*I will give them a heart to know me, that I am the Lord. They will be my people, and I will be their God, for they will return to me with all their hearts.*" In the Gospel of Matthew, 23:37 (NIV), we can almost feel the Savior's anguish at the absence of connection with His people in His words: "*O Jerusalem, Jerusalem, you kill the prophets and stone those sent to you, how often have I longed to gather your children together ... but you were not willing.*"

Perhaps the most poignant expression of God's longing for connection with us is expressed in Matthew 11: 28 (NIV): "*Come to me, all you who are weary and burdened, and I will give you rest.*" Yes, God yearns to connect with us, to establish lines of communication and rituals of communion that draw us into the relationship He intended at creation. Mothers get it. They never give up trying to play a meaningful role in the life of their children, especially their teens. But there is one who is even more invested in connecting, not just with teenagers but with us all. You know Him. We call Him Abba, Father, Sovereign Lord, the Almighty, the one and only God Jehovah.

Stop shrugging your shoulders, thinking you don't need Him in your life. Get connected with the source that gave you that life in the first place. He's waiting for you to turn around and plug in and give Him your attention.

Faith Footprint: Reflect upon the state of your connectedness to the Lord. Have you slipped back into old practices when your connectiveness was shaky, off and on or absent altogether? What can you do to reconnect? If you're not disconnected from God, share what you are doing to maintain that connectiveness.

Chapter Thirty-four

We Can Do Hard

"For God has not given us a spirit of fear; but of power and of love and of a sound mind."

~2 Timothy 1:7 NKJV

The auditorium was packed with parents, grandparents, other relatives and friends that Sunday afternoon in late May at Fayette County's traditional Baccalaureate Service for the soon to be graduates of the local high schools. In some urban school districts throughout the states this religious service held before graduation or commencement to send the graduates off with a "farewell sermon" has vanished from the public-school landscape. But in the southern areas of the nation, it holds forth as a traditional landmark of this developmental passage for students. I'm glad it does. I still can remember at my baccalaureate the seriousness of the event as the student and adult speakers offered encouragement tinged with spiritual wisdom and guidance to bright-eyed, eager, and nervous late teens drawing closer to official adulthood.

This was my youngest granddaughter's time. The pandemic of 2020 had wiped out these gatherings for my oldest granddaughter; we adults were almost as excited as our restless teenagers to see a return to normalcy. After the customary greetings from District officials, principals, senior class sponsors, and other dignitaries, a youth minister spoke to the graduates. The title of his remarks was *"We Can Do Hard."*

He gave the background story for the title. He saw the phrase on the bulletin board of a kindergarten classroom. In conversation with the teacher, she talked about how the typical kindergartener approaches the new experience of going to "real school" with excitement. But somewhere between the great idea of finally being old enough to do so and the realization of what it might mean, doubt makes its way into the five-year-old psychic. At the classroom door, they cling to their parent's hand, their eagerness dampened by the profusion of "learning" tools adorning their new environment. The teacher explained that's why she chose the classroom mantra: "*We Can Do Hard.*" She tells them that "Yes," some things will be hard. But that's okay because they will learn not to be afraid of hard stuff; that together they will do what needs to be done, whether it's hard or not.

The minister pointed out to the graduates they were embarking on a new path and there would be challenges they might think are too hard. But, he said, just as they learned in the twelve years prior, because something appears "hard" does not mean one cannot tackle it and accomplish their goal in so doing.

The message directed to the twelfth graders caused me to reflect upon the Apostle Paul and his young protege, Timothy. The apostle wrote letters (1 and 2 Timothy) to give Timothy encouragement and guidance as he matured in leadership within the church at Ephesus. In the chapter verse, Paul is direct. Timothy must not fall prey to doubt in carrying out his commission, but rather recall that God has given him a spirit of confidence and assurance, not fear or cowardice at the tasks set before him.

We Christians today face twenty-first century dilemmas that appear impossible, and "hard." Too easily we slip into a "kindergartener" mindset. Doubt clouds our thinking, and we become timid, hesitant and unsure of ourselves when faced with them. Like the five-year old, we hang back, not sure we can do this. It's just too hard! Paul answers our doubts and fears today as he did in his counsel to Timothy. God is not stingy. He gives us what He gave Timothy: a spirit of power within our spheres of influence to make a difference when we can, where we can, and in the manner, He allows; to use our minds in His service and the power to choose love, rather than its nemesis in our interactions with His beloved community.

Yes, at a high school baccalaureate service, as He always is, God was in play. A kindergartener's teacher's classroom motto—*We Can Do Hard*—translated into His message for those graduates and all of us that there is nothing too hard for the Lord. And in His Spirit and within His will neither is there for us.

Faith Footprint: Reflect upon the classroom motto, *We Can Do Hard*. Are there areas in your present life experiences in which the message of the motto helps you?

Chapter Thirty-five

You're On the Clock Tic-Tock

"There is a time for everything.…"

~Ecclesiastes 3:1 NIV

"No one knows about that day or hour, … Be on guard! Be alert! You do not know when that time will come."

~Mark 13:32 NIV

"Now, brothers, about times and dates we do not need to write to you, for you know very well that the day of the Lord will come like a thief in the night."

~1 Thessalonians 5:1–2 NIV

On that somewhat warm, end of spring Friday evening at the outdoor commencement of my youngest granddaughter's high school graduation, their principal stood before the podium to deliver her final address to the seniors before the familiar strains of the "Pomp and Circumstance March" filled the air, and they accepted their diplomas. She began her remarks with the comment that what she wanted to say was not what she had originally prepared. She changed her mind following a brief encounter with a parent of one the students at the Baccalaureate service a few days before. As the crowd departed, a parent stopped her to offer kudos for a great service and added, *"You're on the clock,"* as she waved good-by. The comment stuck with her over that weekend and the days leading up to graduation.

She explained to the students that the parent's comment was spoken to remind her that she didn't have much time left to be certain she had handled the upcoming details for the night; that everything had been done to ensure all would go as planned without snafus or disappointments.

To say the quote resonated instantly with me is an understatement. I took out my little note calendar and jotted it down, knowing that in the context of an ordinary human interaction God once again revealed His omnipresence. Throughout the remainder of her speech, she spoke to her "anxious to move on" seniors about the reality of that statement for them as they marked a new chapter in their life. Forever after they too would be "*on the clock*" as college students, joined the work force in their sundry careers, and marched through the decades that were to come.

As a Christian, I reflected that not only were these young people "*on the clock*," so to speak, but so too are believers in God and Christ Jesus. John 9:4 records Jesus saying to His disciples, "As long as it is day, we must do the works of him who sent me. Night is coming, when no one can work." And the Apostle Paul writes in his epistle to the Romans, "Love your neighbor as yourself. Love does no harm to its neighbor. Therefore, love is the fulfillment of the law. And do this understanding the present time. The hour has come for you to wake up from your slumber, because our salvation is nearer now than when we first believed." (Romans 13:9–11 NIV) Believers, as we understand the word of God, march on our journey with divine expectations and directions of how to live to accomplish the goals God sets for us. Time is finite. And within the time we are appointed at birth, the clock starts ticking. During that life span, God's Holy Word gives all the guidance we need to avoid the snafus and pitfalls scattered along the way. If we take heed, when the tic-tock of our destiny ceases one glorious day, we will hear the Master proclaim, "Well done, good and faithful, servant." We will have dotted all the i's and crossed all the t's right on time.

I sat in a stadium chair in the bleachers of a high school football field where my grandchild had cheered her team for three of her four years, and realized God was present in those moments. A simple piece of advice spoken by a concerned parent to the principal revealed His extraordinary presence in the ordinary goings and comings of his creation. We have work to do yet, and when we are sensitive to His Presence in everything, He helps us to get it done to His glory. Who is like Him? Nobody! Where might He show up? Anywhere! Anytime!

Faith Footprint: Reflect upon a particular experience or experiences you've had or noticed in which you know without a doubt that God was present in what some may term mundane ways.

Chapter Thirty-six

Did You Hang Up? Are You Still There?

"I love the Lord, for he heard my voice; he heard my cry for mercy. Because He turned his ear to me, I will call on him as long as I live."
~Psalm 116:1–2 NIV

"I call on you, O God, for you will answer me; and give ear to me and hear my prayer."

~Psalm 17:6 NIV

Earlier in the summer I was on a long-distance call with one of my BFFs (Best Friends Forever). Such calls which I term "phone visits," are always a treat as they lessen the ache of our not being able to hang out in person because of the distance between us. She resides in Los Angeles, my former hometown, and I am in Texas. The calls keep us connected though, and never fail to leave me collapsed in laughter and often tears as she shares her latest life experiences. At some point that day, another friend of ours called her. Because she remains challenged by the features of our smartphones, her attempt to put me on hold, tell the friend she'd call her back, and reconnect with me failed, and inadvertently our call dropped. I was not surprised and waited for her to call back. After her usual "mini rant" about these phones and this technology forced upon us, she settled down and shared that said friend and she very often have a hard time determining if a call made has been answered and if the other can hear her.

"*What,*" I exclaimed!

She proceeded to tell me the common refrain of those calls is

"*Did you hang up?*" or "*Are you still there?*" They say laughter is good for the soul. My soul was sated for sure!

Following our "*good-byes,*" the questions my friends frequently pose to each other floated around in my mind. In the humor of the moment, God pressed. And eventually the thought came. How blessed we are that the very technology God has allowed man to develop exposes who He is; and that all things human will never measure up to His power. Scripture is clear that our Lord's hearing does not fail. Our calls to Him always connect; we need not wonder if He hears us. His ear is more attuned to our voice than any speaking device will ever be. The prophet Isaiah writes of Him, "*Then you will call, and the Lord will answer; you will cry for help, and he will say: Here am I.*" (Isaiah 58:9 NIV) And Romans 10:13 (NIV) reads "*Everyone who calls on the name of the Lord will be saved.*"

Yes, technological advances may have improved, expanded, or simplified much in our everyday lives, but when it comes to communicating with the God who allowed the invention of these devices, miscommunication with Him is a misnomer. As the Holy Word assures us, He never misses a call. No Robocall system decides which ones He will answer. We can never get the wrong number when we say, "*Abba, Father, Hear my pray.*" He picks up and listens to what He already knows we called to talk about. But He hears us out, until our pain becomes His pain and our cry one that only He can answer. Oh, there may be no humor in this call, but the joy of the Lord will overflow filling our souls with sweet relief. He is there and He hears. No technological expertise required for this "phone visit."

Faith Footprint: Do you think of prayer as a time for conversation with God, an opportunity to share what's going on in your life as you understand it? Or is it primarily a time in which you bring your petitions to Him for help and guidance? Which describes you? Can both be looked at in the context of our understanding of communication with God? Reflect and journal your thoughts.

Chapter Thirty-seven

RIDE OR DIE
Stitched at the Hip

"The Lord is near to all who call on him, to all who call on him in truth."

~Psalm 145:18 NIV

"And I will ask the Father, and he will give you another advocate to help you and be with you forever – the Spirit of truth."

~John 14:16 NIV

"… because God has said, never will I leave you; never will I forsake you."

~Hebrews 13:5 NIV

"Then Jesus came to them and said, … And surely, I am with you always, to the very end of the age."

~Matthew 28:20 NIV

Idiomatic expressions have always been part of the social culture of a people. Here in the US, it would be hard to find someone who hasn't heard or uttered at some time or other phrases like, *cost an arm and a leg, beat around the bush, once in a blue moon*, or *the ball's in your court?* Almost ubiquitous, such expressions over the years add flavor to our communication and connectedness to one another. Sometimes even, they define who we are in the context of society.

The chapter title idioms are among the more contemporary ones than the examples given above. I am aware that for some of my gentle readers (those who people the upper regions of the decades), these idioms may be new. That is probably not the case, however, for those yet to reach the half century mark; or for the young at heart who have. I count myself in the latter group. The reference source I used defines "ride or die" as "a colloquial expression indicating extreme loyalty to someone or something, no matter the situation." "Stitched at the hip" is an adaptation of the "joined at the hip" idiom that implies a deep bond, and loyalty.

I first heard "*stitched at the hip*" when my husband's niece used it to describe our marriage. "*Aunt Beverly and Uncle Earl*," she intoned once when were visiting, "are *stitched at the hip. They're always together.*" That phrase stuck. "*Ride or die*" became part of my vocabulary when my youngest grandson was born, a year after Earl had made his departure to live with the Lord. All too soon this little bundle of joy claimed the essence of the first expression and was seldom not near me. As he grew older and I transported him to school, day-care, lessons, games, church activities, wherever, I referred to him as my "*ride or die.*" We were that connected; that close (and still are as often as we can be as he is now in his early teens, and we live in different states).

Recently, I reflected upon how these two contemporary idiomatic expressions apply to my spiritual life; how Jesus and the Holy Spirit are in fact my "ride or die" companions and that we are indeed "stitched at the hip" because we're always together. Whether at home or away, they are the Eternal Ones who fill those roles for me. I expect the Lord to be by my side when I'm driving, taking control of the steering wheel as needed. I know He holds my hand to keep me from stumbling. He whispers in my ear when I'm making decisions, helping me to choose the road He's already laid out for me. He opens doors that are okay to enter or posts a Closed sign on those that are not in His will for me to.

How, you ask, do I know these things and make these claims? As the lyrics of the children's song proclaim, "*For the Bible tells me so.*" Reread the opening scriptures. The Holy Spirit is near to us and with us forever. Jesus himself will never leave us but will be with us forever. That's what "ride or die" and "stitched to the hip" companions do. They stick close; they're always around. They're there with you until the end. You can always count on them. In our heavenly Father, His Son, Jesus and the advocate, the Holy Spirit, we have more than just human companions who do these things. We have the Creator of the world, the Holy Spirit and the Savior of humanity; the Divine Three are the original manifestations of these contemporary expressions. With them in the spaces in our life, we define for the world who we are and whose we are, and why we live as we live.

Faith Footprint: Reflect upon my contention that these idiomatic expressions are applicable to one's relationship with the Lord.

Chapter Thirty-eight

Favor. Favor. Favor.

"For his anger lasts only a moment, but his favor lasts a lifetime…"
~Psalm 30:5 NIV

"For whoever finds me finds life and receives favor from the Lord."
~Proverbs 8:35 NIV

"Jesus grew in wisdom and statue, and in favor with God and man."

~Luke 2:52 NIV

*L*et me say upfront, this is a rather long chapter. I don't apologize though. I think it's a story worth telling and you, gentle reader, hearing.

Six days ago, I received a letter from the Social Security Office. That correspondence set in motion a week of experiences that many might term "coincidences," but I proclaim are proof of God's favor upon and within my life. As is my ongoing contention, the Lord is as present in the ordinary as He is in the extraordinary. The correspondence thanked me for opening an online social security account. In a succeeding paragraph I was cautioned to call the office if I had not initiated this action. I had not. The next day I drove over to the office around midday to discover a packed waiting room and decided to return at an earlier hour the following day.

During the balance of the week, God's favor rested upon me such that I was constantly praising and thanking Him as He blessed me in the midst of mundane events. The chronology of His favor follows:

- Tuesday—As I prepared to leave for the social security office, my car refused to start. Initially, a neighbor and I thought it was my key fob battery. They picked one up for me. The car still refused to start. AAA came, listened to the car as I pressed the brake and ignition and said, "*it's your battery.*" It was dead. When he completed the installation of a new battery, the day was well spent. I decided to wait until the next day to solve the social security mystery. As the beginning of the week at any government office is typically the busiest time, the dead battery spared me the ordeal of what would undoubtedly have been a long day of waiting at the office. That intervention I counted as favor, and I thanked God.

- Wednesday—After signing into the system at the social security office, I took my seat in a sparse crowd, prepared to wait. Within ten minutes or so, a voice called my number. In another five minutes, the worker confirmed the suspended account and said I'd need to speak to someone else regarding what it meant. She said they would call my name. Now, for the long wait, I thought, but within another five minutes, the voice spoke, "*Beverly Clopton, window 3.*" The new clerk and I had an immediate connection—she was wearing a shirt I had purchased at Ross. I so commented and we engaged in a minute of friendly girl-talk before getting to the reason for my visit. After she checked my records, she said someone had attempted to set up the online account and that was the reason for the suspension. It meant that any future online attempts to conduct business by anyone, including me, would be denied. Since I'm not a social security recipient, it didn't matter. I don't have business with them anyway, and if an occasion arose in which I needed to, driving the short distance to their location was no big deal. That was it. In thirty minutes or so, I was in and out of what I'd thought would be an all-day affair. As I walked back to my car, I smiled and said, "favor, Lord, thank you." His extension of it allowed me to proceed to an errand I'd planned for the following day—getting new eyeglasses—before I headed home.

- Thursday—I met a friend from my high school days to celebrate his birthday. Lunch was to be my treat. Two women ahead of us were taking a while to make up their minds when one turned and asked if we would like to go ahead of them. We replied we were still deciding, and I added, "It's his birthday." They turned and offered the usual wishes for a happy birthday. Finally, as they left, they again wished him a happy birthday. The receptionist entered our selections, and then held up a handful of cash. "Your lunch has already been paid for by the ladies who were in front of you; it's their gift for your special day." After totaling the bill that came to over $50, she told me I only owed $11 and change. I said, "Favor." Strangers had blessed my friend whose lunch I was paying for, and through his blessing, I was blessed. Don't tell me that's not God's favor!
- Friday—The preceding days had been so filled with God's favor; surely, I figured, I had received my portion for the week. I was wrong. Following my 30-minute walk in the gym at the senior center, I completed a few errands and headed home. Just as I drove into the garage, a boom of thunder shattered the quietness of the day. The forecast for possible thunderstorms proved true. Rain was on the way, but the car and I were safely out of the elements. Favor on Friday. My Father had one more offering to close out my week. Once again, I said, *Thank you, Lord*,"

Faith Footprint: Take some time to reflect on how and when the Lord has bestowed favor during your ordinary comings and goings. Did you recognize it as such? Did you voice your recognition and thank Him?

Chapter Thirty-nine

THE SQUIRREL

"The Lord is good, a refuge in times of trouble. He cares for those who trust in him."

~Nahum 1:7 NIV

*R*ecently, my sister and I were on the way to the local Parks and Recreation Senior Center for our laps around the gym when without warning, a young squirrel darted in front of my car. Luckily, I saw it before I squashed it, but it was a close call. The little critter didn't know how near it had come to that being its last day among the living. We sat patiently as it froze, looked around and then headed back to the yard from which it had come, scampering up the tree trunk to the safety of the branches. We chuckled at its close encounter with a SUV, wondering if it had any concept of the dangers of crossing a street. We imagined the scolding its mother surely gave it, after first assuring the little one was unharmed. The tiny squirrel had yet to learn that its safety and well-being depended upon two principles of urban survival: staying within the security of the tree branches with its mom and not yielding to the temptation of running off on its own to explore what lay beyond the sanctuary of said tree.

It didn't take long for me to see a connection between the squirrel's behavior and that of many of us. Whether we're babes in faith, or more seasoned, like that little squirrel, we forget from whence comes our security and protection and think we can do things by ourselves. The psalmist declares, "The Lord is my rock, my fortress, and my deliverer; my God is my rock, in whom I take refuge, my shield and the horn of my salvation, my stronghold." (Psalm 18:2 NIV) Too often though, we forget this description of our "tree laden branches," the divine tree that stands as our fortress and from which we receive the wisdom and guidance we need. God is for us what the tree with its branches is for the little squirrel—our protector, our refuge—all we need to avoid being "squashed" by whatever may be coming our way.

And in those seasons when we do scamper away from Him, like the tree that is rooted in its place in the yard, God does not move and neither does He change. He is eternally present, waiting for His wandering flock to realize their errors, their dashes into territories they have no business venturing into. Patiently, like the mother squirrel watching from the branches high in the trees for the little one to realize the street is not where it should be, God watches and waits for His beloved to come to their senses as they recall the words of King David, "For in the day of trouble he will keep me safe in his dwelling; he will hide me in the shelter of his sacred tent and set me high upon a rock." (Psalm 27:5 NIV) As the tree was for the little squirrel who found itself in over its head, danger inches away in the middle of a street it had no business on, so too is our God for us. He "is our refuge and strength, an ever-present help in trouble." (Psalm 46:1 NIV) He is our hiding place and will protect us from trouble and surround us with songs of deliverance. (Psalm 32:7 NIV)

We will never know what made that little squirrel dart out into the street that morning. What we did observe was its sense of where its safety was—in the direction from which it had come, the tree in which we surmise awaited its mother and the security only she could provide. The lesson for us in yet another of God's intrusions into the mundanities of life is simple. "Trust in him at all times ... for God is our refuge." (Psalm 62:8 NIV) If a squirrel can recognize the error of its ways and reverse course, surely, we humans who claim God as our Father and His Son Jesus our Savior can do that and more. God is watching. What better time than now to scamper back to Him?

Faith Footprint: Share how this chapter speaks to you on your faith journey presently. Are you like the little squirrel, dashing into dangers seen or unseen, forgetting the source of your protection and security? Or have you matured in your pursuits such that they align with God's will for your life?

Chapter Forty

LEMONS AND LIFE

"God is our refuge and strength, an ever-present help in trouble. Therefore, we will not fear, though the earth gives way and the mountains fall into the heart of the sea, though its water roar and foam and the mountains quake with surging."

~Psalm 46:1 NIV

Not so long ago in a sermon my pastor posed the question, *"When life squeezes, what comes out?"* As is often the case when a phrase or quote captures my attention, I note it in my "Ideas" book for possible inclusion as a future chapter in a still evolving manuscript. So, here it is. What struck me was the corollary of a common lemon and life, which in and of itself is anything but common.

As we know, the essence of a lemon is accessed by squeezing it. Sometimes it's sliced, but often to get to what's inside it must be squeezed. Because lemons have a high citric acid content, what emerges because of the squeezing is bitter in taste. That's probably why lemon pulp is not an ingredient added to fruit salads. At any rate, the taste of lemons has come to symbolize sourness or some-thing undesirable. Its reputation began back in 1909 when a saying attributed to the writer, Elbert Hubbard, appeared in the *Literary Digest*. *"A genius,"* he wrote, *"is a man who takes the lemons that Fate hands him and starts a lemonade stand."* Over time the little yellow fruit solidified itself as a symbol of something undesirable and the modern-day adage, *"When life gives you lemons, make lemonade,"* came to trip easily off the tongues of old and young alike; a colloquialism understood to reference how we deal with life's difficulties. Squeeze a lemon and you get bitter pulp and sour juice. Squeeze life and the human versions of sourness and bitterness pour forth: despair, anxiety, sorrow, anger, pain, fear, discouragement, and other challenges that test a believer's resolve, strength, and faith.

Because we live in a fallen world, whether we like it or not, there will be squeezing seasons during life's journey. What should the believer do in those times? What should drip from a believer when the pressure tightens? Rather than life's squeezing moments producing those elements noted above, the book we proclaim to be "a lamp unto our feet, and light unto our path" provides the desired responses to our sour moments.

- "… but those who hope in the Lord will renew their strength. They will soar on wings like eagles; they will run and not grow **weary**; they will walk and not **faint**." ~Isaiah 40:31 NIV
- "So do not **fear**, for I am with you; do not be **dismayed**, for I am your God. I will strengthen you and help you; I will uphold you with my righteous right hand." ~Isaiah 41:10 NIV
- "The Lord is good, a refuge in times of **trouble**. ~Nahum 1:7 NIV
- "Do not be afraid; do not be **discouraged**, for the Lord your God will be with you wherever you go." ~Joshua 1:9 NIV
- "Do not be **anxious** about anything…" ~Philippians 4:6 NIV
- "You intended to **harm** me, but God intended it for good to accomplish what is now, the saving of many lives." ~Genesis 50:20 NIV

Scripture drips with assurances and promises which sweetened the sourness and bitterness of life's challenges and difficulties. Whether the pressures of life are self or externally applied, what comes forth is controllable. Unlike the lemon which has no power to affect what gushes forth when its squeezed, we who strive to live in the image of Christ do. Life's "pulps" of weariness, faintheartedness, fear, dismay, trouble, discouragement, anxiety, or harm need not be the issues that emerge; and if by chance they are, God's word offers hope and strength to negate their effect. His word is the sweetener that transforms all bitterness and sourness into comfort, courage, joy, and peace.

Like the lemon we may have little control over why we are selected to be squeezed. But unlike the lemon, we do have a Savior who intercedes for us and operates the best lemonade stand in the universe. He is our Divine Sweetener.

Faith Footprint: What gushes forth from you when life squeezes? Attributes that point to your faith in our God? Or responses more like those who don't know Him as their personal Savior? And if you answer, "a little of both," what do you need to do to address the issue?

Chapter Forty-one

GRACE
Never on Sale. Original Price Only

"God gave the Law through Moses, but grace and truth came through Jesus Christ."

~John 1:16–17 NIV

You've probably at one time or another heard a preacher say that the blessing of grace is not free, that it costs something. That sentiment is not a disclaimer of our understanding that *"grace is the free and unmerited favor of God; manifested in the salvation of sinners."* Yet, we also understand that there is a cost factor at play in the blessing of His grace—the crucifixion of Jesus. That's why grace is not cheap; why at its origin there was a cost.

Perhaps the time of the year brings me to this reflection. In my youth, September heralded "Back to School" time. Today, August ushers in this annual ritual as eager learners head to the hallowed halls of learning fully outfitted with the basic tool of their trade: a backpack (clear ones in this era of campus violence and other unsavory issues that require officials to see what students have in their possession) filled with the necessities required of their grade level. Pre-sales, Three Day Sales, and Final Sales advertisements have abounded leading to their first day back. Parents, guardians and others have searched for the best prices, always with an eye on the cost and what's on sale. Who wants to pay full price for the consumable items that will run out and need to be repurchased as the year moves along? The cost of preparing the scholars for the year's academic endeavors is not cheap.

The Apostle John writes as noted in the chapter scripture that the grace we enjoy as believers in Jesus was provided for us by the price Jesus paid for it—His death on a cross. The original price for our salvation was never marked down; no "50% off the original" flyers plastered the walls along the Via Delarosa. Jesus paid what could not be reduced; the surrender of His life had to be the full price for the grace afforded us by it so we are equipped with the tools we need to work out our salvation. Scripture reminds us in Romans 3:23–25 (NIV) "For we all have sinned and fall short of the glory of God, and all are justified freely by grace through the redemption that came by Jesus Christ. God presented Christ as a sacrifice of atonement, through the shedding of his blood—to be received by faith."

Paul writes in Ephesians 2:8–9 (NIV) "For it is by grace you have been saved, through faith—and this is not from yourselves, it is the gift of God…" No marked down version of grace comes from Jesus' crucifixion. What we have by faith is a backpack filled with what is needed in any circumstance. Does not scripture teach that His grace is sufficient? What we sometimes forget is that His sufficiency so freely given did have an initial price tag attached. That tag read, "Not on Sale—Original Price only."

Maybe the next time we stop for the yellow school bus to take on or let off the future leaders of our world, and we watch them struggle with those hefty packs on their backs, we'll remember that someone who loves and cares for them made the sacrifice to equip them to pursue their learning. Perhaps we will remember in that moment that someone did the same for us thousands of years ago. Jesus stayed on a cross and died to cover the cost of the grace his Father would forever provide us, His children, who every day need it to live as the people of God we proclaim to be, always aware of the cost.

Faith Footprint: As you reflect upon this chapter, ask yourself if you are keenly aware throughout the day of the cost Christ paid for the grace God extends to you. How do you honor that sacrifice?

Chapter Forty-two

Bucket List

"Many are the plans in a person's heart, but it is the Lord's purpose that prevails."

~Proverbs 19:21 NIV

The 2024 Olympics were in full swing one day as I walked inside the gym's basketball court chasing my daily step count. A woman of similar intent caught up with me and introduced herself. As we continued rounding the outer court lines at the same pace, her phone rang. There followed within my hearing a lively conversation having to do with an Airbnb reservation. When she disconnected the call, she smiled and shared that she and a group of family and friends were trying to solidify their reservations in Los Angeles for the 2028 Olympics. I must have blinked because she laughed and responded, "Yeah, it's early but we're planning now. Going to the Olympics is one of the things on my bucket list."

At the time I didn't think much more about our brief conversation, but soon enough, the gist of it blossomed into a chapter title, and here we are. The term "Bucket List" captures a contemporary trend which The Oxford Language Dictionary says was popularized in 2007 by the movie, *The Bucket List*. It refers to the things a person wants to accomplish or to do during his/her lifetime. I admit I have used it myself, especially when referring to places I still yearn to visit. Though at present I'm not caught in the throes of planning such trips as is my walking companion, the desire crouches still in my mind's recesses.

It didn't take long before my mind, wired as it is, to juxtapose the term "Bucket List" with the colloquial phrase, "If you want to make God laugh, tell him your plans." I discovered that idiom can be traced to the comedian Woody Allen and is supposedly an adaptation of a Yiddish saying, "We plan. God laughs." I smiled with the realization that "Ever-Present" was a silent party to that interaction with my walking companion and again had a word for those who are open to the wonder of His presence in the least expected places.

God's guidelines for living abound in the pages of His Word. The wisdom writer of Proverbs succinctly says, "In their hearts humans plan their course, but the Lord establishes their steps." (Proverbs 16:9 NIV) It is a caution verse designed to remind us that our plans often fail to materialize as we wish because we forget to commit them first to the Lord so that He establishes them according to His will and purposes. (Proverbs 16:3 NIV) Because His thoughts and ways are not ours, (Isaiah 55:8 NIV), we run the risk of missing the counsel available to us when we proceed with our plans absent His input and guidance. We must never forget we serve a God who is a promise keeper. The words of the Psalmist are the assurance we have of what God does for those who place their plans and aspirations at His altar in advance of making them, "I will instruct you and teach you in the way you should go; I will counsel you with my loving eye upon you." (Psalm 32:8 NIV) That promise and the one spoken to Jeremiah remain true for us today: "For I know the plans I have for you, declares the Lord, plans to prosper you and not to harm you, plans to give you hope and a future." (Jeremiah 29:11 NIV)

I'm hoping the connection is clear—plans absent God's input and direction may fail to materialize. As we busily scheme to cement them by our own initiative, not pausing to consult He who is sovereign over everything we do, it's not a stretch to imagine Him smiling, if not laughing, at our efforts. Our audacity probably provides Him with a daily chuckle. The lesson, I believe, is simple. When God allows the intellect He gave us to come up with an idea or a plan to do something, before rushing headlong into preparation mode, we must spend time in prayer and reflection first. Ecclesiastes 3:1 is a great thought provoker—"There is a time for everything, a season for every activity." Ask the question of your Counselor, the Holy

Spirit if this is the time to pursue this dream or to commit to this plan? Ask for His guidance before you sign the rental agreement for Airbnb or make the airline reservations. Wait for His answer and proceed accordingly. Remember, "Trust in the Lord with all your heart, and lean not upon your own understanding. In all your ways acknowledge Him and He will direct your path." (Proverbs 3:5–6 NIV) We can drop the mike right here!

Faith Footprint: Reflect upon your planning style. Are you more apt to plan first and ask God's blessings upon the plans afterward? Or are you deliberate in taking everything to God first? The major stuff and the minor stuff? Be honest. Is there some room for improvement in this area of your spiritual journey?

Chapter Forty-three

COMFORT AT QT

"You are my Comforter in sorrow, my heart is faint within me."
~Jeremiah 8:18 NIV

According to QuikTrip.com there are over one thousand of its convenience stores and gasoline pumps spread across the nation in seventeen states. Their familiar logo—QT in a red square—stands high in the sky, easily recognizable. It's a billion-dollar company which, according to the website, donates 5% of their net profits yearly to local charitable organizations. Beyond the typical attractions of such places, i.e., mini store and available restroom facilities, their gas prices are lower than the large gasoline chain distributors. Most times drivers must wait for a free pump station. The lure of the well-kept stores and amenities including inexpensive gasoline is too good to pass up. It's easy to think of QT as the place to stop when traveling, especially when the gas gauge is near E.

Such was the case when I pulled into the station that Sunday in mid-June. It was late morning on Father's Day. Numb with grief after my son made his transition from this earthly dwelling to the eternal home that awaits those who believe in Jesus' promises, I pulled into the familiar station, needing both gasoline and a few minutes of minutiae, as I processed his departure. Though his passing had been anticipated for the past two weeks, the actuality of his spirit no longer being present was heart-wrenching. My grown-man baby was gone. I had enough sense to know that the comfort I needed only God could supply. Quite frankly I had not the slightest notion of how He would, but I knew He would. And it was only after He did, that I realized He had.

As I waited my turn for an open pump, I noticed a bedraggled young woman going from car to car. It appeared she was begging, and I figured she'd get to me in a few minutes. I stepped out before she approached, listened to her story of needing money for gas and food and handed her what I had decided to give. She pointed over to the last row of pumps and identified the car in which she said her mother and daughter waited before she moved on to the next car. A good fifteen or so minutes passed before I finished filling my vehicle and started maneuvering it out of the station. The exit path required me to pass directly by the car in which the mother and granddaughter waited.

The Holy Spirit intervened in that moment; I stopped, rolled down my window and called out, asking if she was the mother of the young woman who was soliciting drivers. She nodded and said, *"Yes, we need gas, and I don't have any money, and she doesn't either and my granddaughter is hungry."* A little person of about four or five years bumped around in the backseat looking out the window at her mom. My heart flipped. My mind did a somersault. In that moment, thoughts of Quentin receded. I supposed my grief decided it needed a break too. At any rate, instead of the hurt that moments before gripped my heart, I instead felt a need to offer more than the five dollars I'd handed over. Waving my hand, I got her attention, and she headed over as I beckoned. Somewhat hesitantly, she approached and was at first skeptical when I said I wanted to fuel their car; and give her additional cash to get food. But no candy, I cautioned as the little girl kept begging for it. Both she and her mom continued to be reluctant to accept my offerings. They kept saying, *"Are you sure? That's a lot of money to fill it up; it's empty. Just a little will be enough. Are you sure?"* Over and over, I replied, "Yes, I'm sure."

By God's grace and favor in that encounter, my focus shifted from me to a small family in need. Why they were was not for me to ascertain. God knew their story as He knew mine. If they were grifters, the Lord would sort it out. I was called to follow His teachings. When I did, He gave me comfort in a manner we seldom think of when the Grim Reaper holds sway. He knew His comfort would be given to me as I gave it to someone else. On the surface, their lack of gasoline and food and my son's death seem to have zero in common. But as I drove away, smiling at the family and they at me—after multiple expressions of "thank you"—I realized the heaviness of heart and numbness of spirit that drove me into QT had vanished. God had brought together the incongruities of those life moments to achieve His purpose, to be as His word proclaims:

- "I, even I, am he who comforts you." ~Psalm 51:12 NIV
- "For the Lord comforts his people and will have compassion on the afflicted ones." ~Isaiah 49:13 NIV
- "Praise be to the God and Father of our Lord Jesus Christ, the Father of compassion and the God of all comfort, who comforts us in our troubles, so that we can comfort those in any trouble with the comfort we ourselves receive from God" ~2 Corinthians 1:3 NIV
- "I have told you these things, so that in me you may have peace. In this world you will have trouble. But take heart! I have overcome the world." ~John 16:33 NIV

At an ordinary place in an extraordinary moment, God once again kept a promise. His comfort and peace will continue to be than sufficient during my sojourn in Grief City. Be on notice though: My day of "taking heart" will have a "restart date."

Faith Footprint: Is there a vivid moment in your life in which you knew without doubt that God's comfort had reshaped how you felt and what you did as a result. Journal or share with a friend as a joy.

Chapter Forty-four

Sin: Repent or Manage

"And Samuel said to the whole house of Israel. "if you are returning to the Lord with all your hearts, then rid yourselves of the foreign gods and the Ashtoreths and commit yourselves to the Lord and serve him only,"

~1 Samuel 7:3 NIV

"God came to John … in the desert. He went into all the country around the Jordan, preaching a baptism of repentance for the forgiveness of sins."

~Luke 3:3 NIV

"This is what the Sovereign Lord, the Holy One of Israel says: In repentance and rest is your salvation, in quietness and trust is your strength, but you would have none of it."

~Isaiah 30:15 NIV

As is my habit, I followed the pastor's sermonic discourse waiting to hear a word I could claim as being meant just for me. Sometimes, in addition to that I also get words that lead to further reflection and then morph into inspiration for my writing. Such was the case recently. He executed a "show and tell" movement, a ninety-degree turn from the direction he was facing, to demonstrate what repenting from sin—aka repentance—looks like. His point was that when we repent, the turn away from sin should resemble a ninety-degree movement rather than a 180-degree one. Coming full circle means we repent, and then go back to the practices we turned away from.

Then, in an aside almost, he stated too many folks have perfected the art of "managing" their sins rather than turning away from them. Simply put, they've mastered the art of what I term "repentance overlaid with maintenance."

If your response right now is, "*Huh?*" stay with me. In practical terms, repentance is two-fold. The Israelites had accepted God as their sovereign one but had strayed from his laws and teachings. Over time, the practices they had once turned from crept back into the culture. Outwardly, they managed to stay connected to God, but their hearts yielded again to desires of the flesh. It was at that juncture Samuel spoke the words noted in our opening scripture. And unfortunately, over the centuries the secular lures of culture continued to negate their original turn from the world to God. Repentance was unsustainable; the ninety-degree turn seemed always to be replaced with a full 180 degree one—sin continued to hold its sway.

Times are no different for us modern day believers. Despite Jesus's words: *"Repent, for the kingdom of heaven has come near,"* (Matthew 4:17 NIV); *"Jesus answered them, 'It is not the healthy who need a doctor, but the sick. I have not come to call the righteous, but sinners to repentance.'"* (Luke 5:32 NIV) We struggle to repent without relapse and have adopted instead the default position of "managing sin." The Oxford Dictionary of Languages notes thirty-one definitions of the word sin. It's a veritable smorgasbord of practices from which supposedly we have turned away. And therein is the rub. Faced with the choice of really abandoning the practices we've repented of, we choose instead to redesign them, to make them fit more within secular perspectives. "What is morality anyway? What makes an act or behavior good or bad? Ungodliness? What does that even mean? So, what if in the heat of the moment profane words slip from my mouth? Everybody curses every now and then, right? What is so awful about wanting a little recognition for what I do for others? I mean, some people don't do anything. Nobody's perfect, right?"

When we find ourselves making excuses for behaviors that we've identified as sinful and outside God's expectations, we have opted for management of sin rather than repentance of it. What can we do, after acknowledging that we're pretty good at "sin management" to turn away from it and reestablish a right relationship with God? Perhaps we approach surrendering to His teachings as we first did when we accepted Him as Lord and Savior of our life. We had idols then; though we didn't think of them as such until after we immersed ourselves in His word and discovered "what says the Lord." More time lingering in the wisdom of holy scripture and less scrolling our phones, tablets or computers can loosen the hold those "idols" have upon us. The same principle can be employed to how we spend our unstructured time pursuing the "idols" of secular activities or how we allocate our resources and resist the "idols" of unnecessary acquisitions in favor of sharing more with the least and last among us. Rather than living as the people of God who are "in the world but not of the world," our identity is compromised. As expert managers of sin, we're like a "twinsie" of the secular. Sadly, we conform to its standards rather than to God's, comfortable with being a sin manager rather than repentant. True repentance leads to transformation with the resulting image of Christ that follows having no desire for the idols to which it once clung.

Faith Footprint: Reflect upon the idea of being sin managers. Do you see yourself in this perspective or are you truly repentant. Talk to God about it and seek His guidance.

Chapter Forty-five

CAP'N CRUNCH

*"Surely God is my salvation; I will trust and not be afraid.
The Lord, the Lord is my strength and my song; He has become
my salvation."*

~Isaiah 12:2 NIV

Once again, in the humor of a comic strip, the presence of God can be sensed beneath its panels and conversation contained therein. Recently I read one such three-paneled strip in which a teenage boy is busy at his computer, desk strewn with books and papers, when his mom appears, notes his industriousness, and asks, *"Research?"* He responds that he's working on an assignment in which he must write a paper on a fictional character who has had an impact upon him. Peering over his shoulder in the last panel, Mom looks at his computer screen and says, *"Cap'n Crunch?"* Son replies, *"He's gotten me through a lot of Saturday mornings."* It was the chuckle for the day that I'm always on the lookout for as I am a firm believer that laughter is good for the body and soul, as scripture confirms in Proverbs 17:22 NIV: "A cheerful heart is good medicine, but a crushed spirit dries up the bones."

Just in case you are unfamiliar with the name, Cap'n Crunch, it's a trademark cartoon character of a sweetened breakfast cereal that is a stable in the diet of many young people, especially teenagers. As I am no longer the cartoon "glancer" I was when my son and later my grandkids were growing up, glued to the television on Saturday mornings, I'd forgotten how enamored they can become to the parade of cartoon characters who promote the products that sponsor those shows, Cap'n Crunch among them.

Soon enough though my laughter faded as I focused on the teenager's comment that a cartoon character had gotten him through many Saturday mornings. Now what our teenager needed "getting through" during his formative years only the Lord knows. Whatever it was, he credited a fictional character for helping him with it. His statement struck a chord. Within it I could see a definite analogy. Whereas His rescuer was a fictional cartoon character, our "Cap'n Crunch" (if I'm allowed the liberty of literary license to so describe Him) is anything but fictional. Quite the opposite in fact—He's the real deal who gets us through not just on Saturday morning, but every morning He awakens us. He's the One who was present at creation and participant in all that followed. He is the Son of God and the Son of Man who sacrificed His life to restore us to right relationship to His Father and Ours. He sits at God's right hand, interceding on our behalf, i.e. getting us through the myriads of challenges life offers up. We call Him Jesus, Holy Father, God Almighty. He sets the standard for "getting folk through." But don't take my word for this assertion. Let Scripture speak for itself:

> *"The name of the Lord is a strong tower; the righteous run to it and are saved."*
>
> ~Proverbs 18:10 NIV

> *"I will strengthen you and help you; I will uphold you with my righteous right had."*
>
> ~Isaiah 41:10 NIV

> *"Then Moses stretched out his hand over the sea... and the Lord drove the sea back. ... The waters divided, and the Israelites went through the sea on dry ground, ..."*
>
> ~Exodus 14:21–22 NIV

> *"My grace is sufficient for you, for my power is made perfect in weakness. ... That is why, for Christ's sake, I delight in weaknesses, in insults, in hardships, in persecutions, in difficulties. For when I am weak, then I am strong."*
>
> ~2 Corinthians 12:9–10 NIV

"Do not be anxious about anything, but in everything, by prayer and petition, present your requests to God."

~Philippians 4:6 NIV

Underneath the levity of the teenager's comment is a message worthy of thought. We all need something or someone to help us when storms rage, support systems falter or fail, test results bring us to our knees, the grim reaper stops at our door. May these scriptures and others sprinkled throughout God's Holy Word remind us that that Someone is the eternal God who created us and is the source of what we need to sustain us, to get through the "going-through" seasons of life. He's the Captain in any situation that needs some Crunch!

Faith Footprint: The teenager's comment gives pause for reflection, or if you'll pardon the pun, "something to chew on." Are there areas in your life where you have allowed secular influences to substitute for God's provision and promises? Perhaps now is a good time to attend to this breach in your relationship with Him regarding them.

Chapter Forty-six

On the Other Side of the Street

"On one occasion an expert in the law stood up to test Jesus. 'Teacher,' he asked, 'what must I do to inherit eternal life?' 'What is written in the Law?' he replied. How do you read it?' He answered, 'Love the Lord your God with all your heart and with all your soul and with all your strength and with all your mind and love your neighbor as yourself.' 'You have answered correctly,' Jesus replied. 'Do this and you will live.' But he wanted to justify himself, so he asked Jesus, 'And who is my neighbor?'"

~Luke 10:25–29 NIV

The front page of last Sunday's Opinion section in the local newspaper immediately caught my attention. The starkness of the message within the drawing was sobering. Beneath a beautiful blue sky scattered with fluffy white clouds sat a neighborhood street. On one side of the street's double white line stood impressive two-story brick homes with well-tended lawns, shrubbery and trees towering behind. Directly across from them a row of tents usually seen in areas where the unhoused live dotted the length of the block. Outside the tents trash littered the area. Upon the blue space of the sky was written: "*A Dallas City Council member says city's approach is failing and calls for a better balance of tough enforcement and compassionate aid.*" Speaking of an artist's ability to capture the essence of a moment, a situation, whoever drew this picture did just that. A solution to the urgency of resolving this humanitarian societal issue remains elusive. Stop gap measures abound in every form. Yet, the beat goes on. When asked, most of us acknowledge it's a problem, but also, we admit quicky, one that we don't have an answer for.

As I sat stared at the drawing, the parable of The Good Samaritan that Jesus told to the expert in the Law came to mind. It's familiar to many, but to those for whom it's not, I'll summarize. The chapter verse above preceded Jesus' telling the story of a destitute man who had been robbed, left wounded and in need on a commonly walked road. As the man lay there, both a priest and a Levite (someone who performs subordinate services in a Jewish worship service), came upon him. Neither stopped to offer aid. Instead, they crossed to the other side. Eventually, as it happened, a Samaritan, a member of the sect of Judaism at odds with that of the wounded Jewish man, stopped and helped him, going above and beyond meeting his needs. At that point in his dialogue, Jesus posed a simple question to the expert in the law, "Which of these three do you think was a neighbor to the man who fell into the hands of robbers?" The expert's response, "The one who had mercy on him." At which point, Jesus responded with words that are an echo to us today, "Go and do likewise."

I want to keep this real. When I look at the picture referenced above, I identify with the residents who live in the brick homes with the well-tended lawns and beautiful flowers. To imagine looking from my window at rows of tents occupied by folks who have not the means, nor perhaps the will to live anywhere else is nightmarish. Now, I imagine most of you who are reading this are not faced with the immediacy of homelessness or as it's more politically correct to say, "unhoused" persons as the drawing I've described suggests. Your experiences are like mind for the most part: seeing such "housing"— tents, cardboard boxes, blankets strung across whatever will support them—on the news, on nonresidential streets, underneath the freeway or bridges, under trees in public spaces. But if I'm honest, I admit when I do come upon such scenes of need, my immediate reaction mirrors more the priest and Levite than the Samaritan.

I don't know about you, but I console myself by giving often to non-profit organizations that address and meet the needs of the unhoused; by keeping a donation box in my car to take to a local shelter when it's filled with the overflow from my closet. Yet, this niggling feeling of failing to truly demonstrate neighborliness to those in need or who can't return it, weighs upon me. Jesus' directive is simple, clear. It demands only obedience to it.

Even as the societal forces that contribute to this issue appear beyond our control to reign in, Jesus' example to us remains. Oh, we may not be at the table in places where decisions are made one way or another; but at the street level, when we come across the least, the last, the lost, the victim, we can pull out our "Samaritan" robe and offer help within our means to so do. To go an extra mile, to sacrifice, to deny ourselves, to be inconvenienced to "Go and do likewise."

> *"Lord, when did we see you hungry or thirsty or a stranger or needing clothes or in prison, and did not help you?" He will reply, 'I tell you the truth, whatever you did not do for one of the least of these, you did not do for me.'"*
>
> ~Matthew 44–45 NIV

Faith Footprint: Engage in conversation within your friendship and family groups or beyond how we as individuals might help reshape the issue of being unhoused within the framework of our faith.

I Was—She/He Was—We Were

"Behold I am doing a new thing; now it springs forth, do you not perceive it? I will make a way in the wilderness and rivers in the desert."

~Isaiah 43:19 NIV

I spent the middle of the day visiting a cultural museum with a classmate from my high school years who is a couple years my senior. We met at the entrance and proceeded with guides in hand to wander the current exhibits. A few I had seen on visits before, but several were new. As we made our way slowly through them, our conversation was liberally sprinkled with past tense verb forms. "I wasn't born then." "She was the first …." He helped us when …." "Those were the times when there were laws that forbade us to do that." "I recall when that was what we …"

On my drive home, I reflected on how often we made references to the things of the past, the cruelties of a historical period, the cultural norms that were racially biased, unequal, and the outright non-Christlike attitudes and behaviors that defined those who practiced them. Those of us who have been blessed to live well past the mid-century mark, enjoying God's blessings as our sexagenarian, septuagenarian and octogenarian years have had, or are having their turn on stage, live too often in the past, rather than finding new purpose in the season in which we live now.

The writer of Lamentations 3:22–23 NIV reminds us that, "The steadfast love of the Lord never ceases; his mercies never come to an end; they are new every morning…" I see in that promise an invitation to all who still draw breath to seek opportunities to extend mercy and grace in our encounters, our time commitments, our relationships as God so extends new mercy to us each day.

The past behaviors of mankind's inhumanity to man did not reflect the character of Jesus; just as many of the current do not. But settling because we're aging is not an option for believers in Christ, our Savior. As God continues to do new things to bring about His purposes embedded in our creation, we too—irrespective of age—must do the same. We are his hands, his feet, his voice in the world. And there are issues galore needing our attention daily. Now, I could be wrong, but somehow, I don't think He'll be accepting the excuse that we turned away from trying to address them because we grew older. No, this octogenarian mind believes My senior colleagues and I must move from nostalgic reminiscing to active engagement in today's world for as long as our Father God gives us what we need to do so. Laying the past to rest and joining a movement for the future may just earn you that declaration we all yearn to hear, "Well done, good and faithful servant."

Faith Footprint: If you are sixty or older, what is your take on this reflective piece? Would you describe yourself as "still in the struggle" in a definitive way? Or have you settled into this season content with what you've done and no longer interested in "new things" related to kingdom work? Be honest in your assessment.

Chapter Forty-eight

Shaken, Not Stirred

"The end of a matter is better than its beginning, and patience is better than pride. Do not be quickly provoked in your spirit, for anger resides in the lap of fools."
~Ecclesiastes 8–9 NIV

"... for man's anger does not bring about the righteous life that God desires..."
~James 1:20 NIV

"Cast all your anxiety on him because he cares for you."
~1 Peter 5:7 NIV

Yet again my trusty comics offer not such smiles and chuckles, but a reminder of what it means to practice the faith we profess to anyone who is on the lookout for God everywhere. Whether or not just allusions are intended by the authors may be up for debate, but I receive them as a sign that the Almighty dibble-dabbles in all things within His world, including comic strips.

Such is the case with a recent one in which the local bookstore in a small town is set afire. It's the second such incident in the comic strip of book burning. The owner, an astute senior citizen, offers to provide shelf space for books that had been banned from the library and schools so students could have access to them. The evening following the books being shelved, the store is set fire. She was awake when it started and able to summon the fire department before all was destroyed. As several neighbors stand with her surveying the damage, one asks how long she thinks she'll be closed until things are back together. She responds, *"Oh, I'm not closing. I'm shaken but not stirred."*

If you're a fan of the James Bond movie franchise, you're probably familiar with the catchphrase, "shaken, not stirred." It's his classic request whenever he orders a martini. And while for the character of the movie, the phrase sets him apart and speaks to his supposed sophistication, in its more idiomatic usage, according to the Collins dictionary, it references someone who is slightly disturbed by an experience, but not enough to change their behavior or thinking. Such is Lillian, the bookstore owner, who in subsequent days refused to allow the incident to shut down her store.

The analogy was a no-brainer. Life is filled with problems and challenges that test our faith; that reveal who we are and to whom we belong. We may not have had our businesses torched because we choose to carry items that others disapprove of as did the comic strip proprietor. But all of us have faced and some may be in the midst of facing now situations with the potential to shatter us; to alter our confidence, to bring us to our knees—lay-offs in the workplace as your oldest prepares to leave for college; a call from an elderly parent that she's been diagnosed with dementia and can no longer live alone; a rebellious teenager who ignores your rules and comes and goes as he pleases; long-time friends betraying confidences; a schism in your church family; a spouse of twenty-odd years asking for a divorce; the imaging results from your physician confirming your worst nightmare; the news so fraught with violence, discord, misery, corruption in high and low places; mistreatment of the most vulnerable amongst us; environmental disasters; wars and divisiveness. The list of societal ills multiplies daily. How do we respond? What do we do? Give up? Fold? Build a doomsday bunker and go underground? Go on the offense and become part of the problem rather than a seeker of solutions? Open the door and give anxiety, depression, despair, negativity a seat at your table?

Followers of Jesus Christ know those choices are nowhere in their faith toolbox. Instead they pull out as the bookstore owner's comment suggests she did, the courage and conviction inherent in their trust in God's sovereignty. At the initial onslaught of trials or tribulations, there may be a little "shaking" in their posture, but it doesn't progress any farther than that. Nothing "stirs" them into behaviors more commonly associated with nonbelievers. No wailing, no wringing of hands, no bemoaning their fate. No "Where is God?" Their faith in Him is solid, intact and alive. Nothing disturbs or "stirs" it. Like the ever-assured James Bond character, they stand at life's bars surveying the landscape; confident that the hand God has allowed them to be played will in the end be for their good and His glory.

"I can do everything through him who gives me strength."
~Philippians 4:13 NIV

"And we know that in all things God works for the good of all those who love him and have been called according to his purposes."
~Romans 8:28 NIV

Faith Footprint: Reflect upon how you typically respond to bad news. Are you thrown into a tailspin? Unsure of how to handle what needs handling? Desperate? Or are you the more "shaken but not stirred" type?

Chapter Forty-nine

TIME

"Show me, O Lord, my life's end and the number of my days; let me know how fleeting is my life."

~Psalm 39:4 NIV

"Teach us to number our days aright, that we may gain a heart of wisdom."

~Psalm 90:12 NIV

"There is a time for everything, and a season for every activity under the heaven."

~Ecclesiastes 3:1 NIV

I am a long-time fan of PBS broadcasting and an avid viewer of its *Masterpiece* mysteries. One of the reasons I enjoy the channel is the brevity of their commercials. Of the few that do air, one in particular captures my attention. It promotes traveling throughout Europe as something everyone should do. The dulcet tones of the spokesman proclaim that *"the only thing we never have enough of is time,"* and that *"time is a scarce commodity."* He concludes his spiel by advising viewers to use this scarce commodity wisely, further suggesting that there is no better way to do that than to continue to educate ourselves and broaden our minds by traveling to new places.

The commercial is seductive I'll admit, and I always agree with him as I am myself hooked on travel abroad. I can see myself in the places the commercial takes us to, enjoying what the people, i.e., actors, are enjoying; all the while considering when I'll get the time to make it a reality.

On one level the commercial is right. Time is a scarcity. At this very moment we have no idea how much of it remains in our life account. Just this morning its fleetingness struck me anew as I noticed the page marker ribbons in two of my devotional books. Fewer are the pages remaining to be read than when the year began, and the ribbon was laid after January second. The days ahead seemed so abundant. But the month of October is just two days away, and another year is packing, almost ready to bide us adieu. So, I concur with the dulcet voiced spokesperson, time is a scarce commodity fleeting before our eyes, and we should use wisely what we have of it as each twenty-four hours passes.

But it is the suggestion he intones about how to accomplish that which gives me pause. On the surface, there is nothing inherently wrong or ill-advised about continuing to educate oneself, nor seeking to broaden one's mind. And if traveling is a way to do that, I say go for it. But if such pursuits are strictly for secular purposes, I believe anyone who professes belief in God and Jesus Christ His Son rejects this secular understanding of the wise use of time. Perhaps more than others, we understand the concept of time differently. Our Holy Bible clarifies for us what God's expectations are for us relating to it. In addition to the introductory scriptures, reflect for a moment on the following passages:

- "Blessed is the man who finds wisdom, the man who gains understanding, for she is more profitable than silver and yields better returns than gold." ~Proverbs 3:13 NIV
- "My son, do not forget my teachings, but keep my commands in your heart, for they will prolong your life many years and bring you prosperity." ~Proverbs 3:1 NIV
- "Be very careful then, how you live—not as unwise but as wise, making the most of every opportunity, because the days are evil." ~Ephesians 5:15–16 NIV
- "Devote yourselves to prayer, being watchful and thankful. ... Be wise in the way you act toward others... Let your conversation be always full of grace." ~Colossians 2, 5–6 NIV

- "Who is wise and understanding among you? Let him show it by his good life, by his deeds done in humility that comes from wisdom, ... the wisdom that comes from heaven is first of all pure; then peace-loving, considerate, submissive, full of mercy and good fruit, impartial and sincere." ~James 3:13–17 NIV

A believer's response to the question, "What better way to spend our time than by traveling and continuing to educate ourselves and broaden our minds?" veers at this point from a secular perspective to a sacred one. We understand our life's purpose is not to just satisfy fleshly desires, but rather to obey God's call of pointing others to Him. Therefore, we embrace the scarcity of time by pursuing the wisdom inherent in His word so that we might be a beacon to others. We equate the knowledge we gain in study of His teachings as important as that in our secular undertakings. We count the time spent in Bible study sessions, devotional reading, communal and individual worship as crucial to the expansion of our understanding of how to live a Christian life in a fallen world. If travel augments this primary pursuit, we embrace it as much if not more than we do our secular excursions. We purposely use the time we cannot count as wisely as possible each day. We understand any day can be the day when our time runs out, expires, and our purpose fulfilled or not.

Oh, others may not think too highly of these sacred expenditures of time as wise investments in it, but that's okay. We'd rather be found "on the battlefield for the Lord" any time of the day than be held accountable on that Great Day of Accountability for thinking a boat ride on the Seine River or browsing the Louvre is what He meant by using our time wisely.

After thought: Hedge your bet. Get all the educating and broadening you can afford but get even more of Jesus. Seriously, He's the eternal supreme mind broadener.

Faith Footprint: Your thoughts? How would you describe your current use of time knowing that it is scarce and may end without notice.

Chapter Fifty

Because Q Lived
Joy Within the Sorrow

"… weeping may stay for the night, but rejoicing comes in the morning."

~Psalm 30:5 NIV

"Now is your time of grief, but I will see you again and you will rejoice, and no one will take away your joy."

~John 16:22 NIV

As I've stated throughout the previous chapters, my desire has been to highlight that God is omnipresent and engages us in the commonplace rhythms of our lives, hoping that we will sense Him. Originally, this last chapter was to show how He was doing that in the life of my only son, Quentin, as he continued to reside in a long-term facility because of a stroke he'd suffered in 2016. "Q" as he was called by many (excepting me as I called him "Sonshine" during that season and the moniker stuck), was moving toward his eighth year there when God threw a monkey wrench into what had become his and our norm. Unexpectedly, the night following an ordinary virtual visit during which he was fine (if you can term "fine" within his reality of being immobile, voiceless, and totally dependent upon others for his basic needs), paramedics rushed him to ER. Subsequently, he spent over a month in ICU, eventually transferring to a Long-Term Acute Care Hospital. It would be from that facility that he would make a final move—from his earthly home to his eternal one. It took four months.

At this writing, I and others of Quentin's immediate family and close friends are still processing the streets of Grief City. Simultaneously, the Holy Spirit is helping me see that though Grief/Sorrow might seem to be leading the procession, Joy is the Grand Marshall setting the tone as we march behind. In some ways this poem by Robert Browning Hamilton, which I discovered in the devotional book, *Streams in the Desert*, reminded me of that:

> *I walked a mile with Pleasure,*
> > *She chattered all the way;*
> *But left me none the wiser*
> > *For all she had to say.*
> *I walked a mile with Sorrow,*
> > *And ne'er a word said she;*
> *But oh, the things I learned from her*
> > *When Sorrow walked with me.*

Though from a secular perspective, Quentin's life may have seemed exhausted of what we term "living," within it nonetheless God was teaching and equipping us to be the people of faith we proclaim to be. Pure treasures are those moments with Q engaging in one-sided conversations, listening to music, or watching movies, reading scriptures, devotional excerpts, or the newspaper; singing, walking down memory lane looking at pictures on the phone or photo albums that burst forth now into memories that are lessening the pain of his transition. As he responded with the nodding or shaking of his head, or sometimes a guttural sound, joy filled our time and space as we learned together to allow God's spirit and His word to set the tone for the season we were in. Over time, our in-person or virtual visits with him strengthen us. And eventually what had begun as sorrow and pain and regret over the hand he had been dealt, was transformed into acceptance that God was in control. That acknowledgement freed him and us from despair, hopelessness, or sadness. In their place hope sprang, trust thrust its chest, faith spread its wings, and joy did a happy dance. All because my child lived. An unconventional eight years for sure, but eight years that matured our collective faith such that we can ask the question the Apostle Paul penned in 1 Corinthians 15:55 NIV, *"Where, O death is your victory: Where, O death is your sting?"* and proclaim the answer of our faith. Death had been bested by the cross. Our joy from that certainty of our faith stifled sorrow's sting, and Joy triumphed in my son's life and ours. Because he lived, we can tweak the words of an old gospel song and proclaim: "Because Q lived, we can face today and tomorrow not bound by sorrow as we make our way through this temporary place I term "Grief City." Instead, the sadness of life without him flees, as we allow the memories of him to take their place. We are grateful for his having lived with us, and even more grateful to have him safely in his eternal home, awaiting our reunion with him. He has joined our "great cloud of witnesses." Joy vanquishes Sorrow once again.

> *"Consider it pure joy, my brothers and sisters, whenever you face trials of many kinds, because you know that the testing of your faith produces perseverance."*
> ~James 1:11–13 NIV

> *"Be joyful in hope, patient in affliction, faithful in prayer."*
> ~Romans 12:12 NIV

Faith Footprint: Share your reflections on this response to the inevitability of death and the subsequent sorrow that usually accompanies it.

Acknowledgements

"Trust in the Lord with all your heart and lean not on your own understanding; in all your ways acknowledge him and he will make your path straight."

~Proverbs 3:5–6 NIV

I began the year 2024 with the publication of book six, *Lingering in the Word,* and I am grateful to God for allowing me to end it with book seven, *God in the Commonplace,* ready for the publisher. Without the prompting and inspiration of the Holy Spiri, I would not be continuing to write. So, as is my practice I proclaim, "To God Be the Glory" for allowing me to use the gift of wordcraft He gave me to give back to Him via Christian-themed devotional books, in the hope that others will grow in their faith journey.

As has become the norm, I am joined again in this venture by my "sbam" (sister by another mother) Ann Lloyd who serves as my listening ear. As is her practice she listens to me read the chapters as they are completed. On the lookout for biblical blunders or suggesting scriptures to enhance the theme, she provides what all writers need—a critical listener. I am pleased to say she always has just the right suggestion or a thought I might not have considered. As she knows, I am forever grateful for her support. Team A&B in the house again.

It goes without saying, but I'll say it anyway, I am thankful for my immediate and extended family members, and the tons of sister-friends and friends and friends of friends who purchase and read my books as part of their faith walk. This year I'd like to give a special shout-out to Hannah's Descendants, CWIP Inc, a nationwide prayer ministry founded in 2001in Los Angeles, California, by now retired UMC pastor, Rev. Dianna Masters for selecting my last book, *Lingering in the Word*, for their Lenten Study in 2024; and the Women's Bible Study classes and their pastor at Christian Stronghold Church in Dallas, Texas for selecting that same book for their Fall 2024 Bible Study.

As noted in the final chapter, my son, Quentin, rests with the Lord now, but I am forever indebted to him for the pure joy of being his mother and the blessings of God that flowed though him for forty-three years. His legacy of my grandchildren, the "Grand Four": Logan, Jordan, Brooklin, and Quentin Kristopher Earl Clopton are God's gifts that keep on giving. I am blessed to be their Nyanya.

Once again, I am grateful to my editor and publisher, Mike Parker, at Wordcraft Press for our continuing affiliation, his faith in my writing efforts; and encouragement and patience.

Beverly ND Clopton
Dallas, Texas
October 2024

*B*everly ND Clopton is the eldest of nine children. She grew up in Dallas and completed her undergraduate studies in the great state of Texas before she embarked on a 40-year calling as a professional educator in the Dallas, Denver, and Los Angeles public school systems.

Stepping into retirement offered Beverly the opportunity to return to her first loves—the written word and the Word of God.

She has since published numerous books of essays and devotionals, including *Heaven or Bust: Journey to Glory, Sonshine: Reflections of Faith, Surviving Pitfalls on the Path, Rigors of the Call, Until I Die: Reflections and Tales* and her most recent book, *Lingering in the Word: a 40 Day Devotional.*

www.ingramcontent.com/pod-product-compliance
Lightning Source LLC
Chambersburg PA
CBHW030304130626
46549CB00002B/683